In the Clouds
Above Baghdad

On Patrol

In the Clouds Above Baghdad
Recollections of the R.F.C.
in Mesopotamia during the
First World War against the Turks

J. E. Tennant

In the Clouds Above Baghdad
Recollections of the R.F.C.
in Mesopotamia during the
First World War against the Turks
by J. E. Tennant

First published under the titles
In the Clouds Above Baghdad

Leonaur is an imprint
of Oakpast Ltd

Copyright in this form © 2009 Oakpast Ltd

ISBN: 978-1-84677-744-8 (hardcover)
ISBN: 978-1-84677-743-1 (softcover)

http://www.leonaur.com

Publisher's Notes

In the interests of authenticity, the spellings, grammar and place names
used have been retained from the original editions.

The opinions of the authors represent a view of events in which he
was a participant related from his own perspective,
as such the text is relevant as an historical document.

The views expressed in this book are not necessarily
those of the publisher.

Contents

Foreword	9
Eastwards	11
A Land of Sand, Sun and Sorrow	24
The Battles That Won Baghdad	49
Baghdad and Beyond	91
Days Grave and Gay	132
On Three Fronts	165
A Last Crowded Hour	204

The Moving Finger writes; and, having writ,
Moves on; nor all Thy Piety and Wit
Shall lure it back to cancel half a Line,
Nor, all thy Tears wash out a Word of It.
—Omar.

To Mark, My Brother

Foreword

As I write this it is almost two years to a day since: the date-palms of Fao slipped under the horizon and the steamer steadied on her course down the Gulf. The white torment of the desert is replaced by the view of a London square in Spring; life is respectable and comfortable—and safe. The majority of us who have survived the war are no doubt doomed to die in our beds; when that moment arrives how we shall envy that gay company who went before, sword in hand and faces to the enemy, flower of a generation who with Time are gradually forgotten. Meanwhile we, their old companions, will not forget; we work, play, and make new friends, but we do not forget those gentlemen of England.

It seems a long time since we fought for very existence, so long that to perpetuate my recollections of the campaign in Mesopotamia I have woven these few records together for my own interest; it is neither Military Work nor Literary Aspiration, but perhaps will bring back memories of stirring times to those who served with me. If any other reader peruse these pages, the honour I esteem; for the penmanship I apologise.

J. E. T.

London,
April, 1930.

MESOPOTAMIA

CHAPTER 1

Eastwards

Ah, my Beloved, fill the Cup that clears
Today of past Regrets and future Fears—
Tomorrow? Why, Tomorrow I may be
Myself with Yesterday's Sev'n Thousand Years.

—Omar.

It was the last day of June in 1916 when the shore folk thronged their windows and housetops to wave us farewell, and the roar of cheering and hoots of sirens from the ships in harbour echoed across the water and faded away as we gradually drew out to sea. A destroyer slipped into station on either bow, a throb in the ship told of increased speed, and we were out in the silence and evening mist of the Channel. That night the wireless droned of the storm-burst on the Somme; of the waves of great Englishmen going over the top kicking a football in front of them; of the British pack pressing forward to the sound of a hunting horn—of Hell let loose.

We? Destiny had beckoned us East to fight in a remote land far from the mad swirl of the Western Front, and to those of us who had drunk deep of the wet, cold, squalor, and desolation between the Sea and the Somme, this new venture was a relief. Roving is part of the heritage of our race.

A zigzag course was steered all the way to Port Said, for the Mediterranean was a thickly-infested sea, and many of our predecessors had gone to the bottom. The sea was calm, and they were hot, idle days; the wonderful nights, with sickle moon and lamp-like stars, were fitter background for Love than lurking Tragedy. The old *Jupiter*, shade of a former Channel Fleet, and *Espiègle*, reminder of training days at Dartmouth, lay anchored at Port Said; the war had resurrected many a good old ship. It was odd, after previous acquaintance with this hot, dusty town, to see flying machines come swooping over the ship into the harbour. Forty miles away, at El-Arish, sat the Turkish Army in sullen immobility, having failed in their attempt to invade Egypt; the British line lay along the Canal, on which thousands of troops were encamped, from Suez to Port Said. A great general remarked that during this period the Canal was defending the troops, instead of the troops defending the Canal.

All that stifling July night we were passing British encampments; many of the Tommies were floating about in the Canal, trying to get cool, even at 1 a.m. All night a fusillade of questions passed between ship and shore; the details aboard were anxious to find out if any battalions of their own units were ashore. In answer to their questions "Any Welshmen?" "Any Leicesters?" from the dimness of the banks would come a weary attempt at cheerfulness, "Any beer?" The men on shore seemed to feel forgotten in the desert, and weary of waiting for the action that never came their way. Far on in the night, in the silence of the "wee sma' hoors," a voice rang out from the desert in accents unmistakable, "Is there onybody there fra' Broomielaw?" a breath from home.

The next morning we passed the last British soldier on the bank, a solitary figure in helmet, shorts, and shirt-sleeves, surrounded by the shimmering white plain. A friendly soul on board cried out: "Stick it!" a fitting farewell with the thermometer at 100 deg. Fahr., but his reply to us was: "You'll never come back."

Steaming down the Gulf of Suez, the sun set in a fiery glow behind the Egyptian hills, and the night came as a benediction with the moon nearly full. I sat smoking on deck under the stars, and thought of the little *shikari* Fetieh ibn Sabeah and the ibex we had hunted together four years before among the high tops

In the Mediterranean

of Sinai, just visible on the port bow. The days of peace and sport seemed so many years ago.

The Red Sea proved no disappointment; the *Briton* had not been built for these climates; the saloon at meals was like an inferno, and it was too hot to sleep. The stokers were white men, and unable to carry on unsupported, so forty volunteers were called for, and the Welsh Fusilier ex-miners responded. The temperature of the sea rose to 92 deg. Fahr., and the atmosphere was soaking. The second afternoon the ship's doctor died of heatstroke; we buried him over the poop next morning in a thick haze of heat. The human frame could stand little more; the perspiration ran from head on to deck and down legs into boots.

No sooner had we buried the doctor than one of the crew went down outside my cabin; his clothes were taken off, and we put him close to the side of the ship to get any air there might be, but despite all efforts he was gone in two hours. Such is the Red Sea in July.

We steamed through Hell's Gate on the fifth morning, and by nightfall were off Aden and cooling down. The South-West monsoon, with a tumbling sea and rain squalls, blew fresh life into the ship and bucketed us into Bombay harbour twenty-two days out from Plymouth.

Bombay is unpleasant at the height of the monsoon. The rain lashes down on to the pavement and rises up in steam; an electric fan at night just keeps one dry. The drafts on board disembarked for Poona and Kirkee, there to acclimatise before going up the Gulf. The place at this time was a busy base for the forces up the Persian Gulf and in East Africa, and was not lacking in lurid details of either. There seemed to be little encouraging about Force D. General Gorringe had gone home for an enquiry; sixty *per cent,* of the force were sick and 15,000 invalided out of the country in June; half rations at the front due to insufficient transport; and new river transport despatched from Calcutta by sea, instead of being shipped in sections, had either gone to the bottom in the monsoon or been forced to return for repairs; no fresh food; our cheerful friends gave us a month in the country.

On Tuesday, July 25th, in company with 1,600 Indian troops and their goats and forty Indian army officers, we set sail in the B. I. steamer *Ellenga* for this promised land. We called at Muscat, a god-forsaken looking spot on the south-east coast of Arabia, and an old headquarters of piracy, slave traffic, and gun-running. It was an important Portuguese naval station early in the seventeenth century, but attained its greatest prosperity under Arab rule two hundred years later. Abdul Rezak left on record here in 1442 that *the heat was so intense that it burned the marrow in the bones, the sword in its scabbard melted like wax, and the gems which adorned the hilt of the dagger were reduced to coal. In the plains the chase became a matter of perfect ease, for the desert was filled with roasted gazelles*!

Muscat is picturesque and mediaeval, with its watch towers and large fort commanding the bay, but, as usual, no shade or vegetation to be seen anywhere. Here we left a detachment of the 108th Native Infantry, as, although nominally independent, the Sultan had appealed to the British for protection against the Turk and hostile tribes, to whom his Hinterland was exposed. There had been fighting here in 1915, the Indian garrison having defeated and driven off three thousand Arabs. Little did the British public, more immediately affected by the greater wars, realise how forgotten British officers were dying in nameless fights, or rotting with fever in distant outposts, *unknown, uncared-for, and unsung.*

The heat of the Persian Gulf was as the heat of the Red Sea: the temperature of the water reached 100 deg. Fahr., and one grew weary for want of sleep. At Bushire, a Persian town on the edge of low-lying desert, lay H.M.S. *Juno*, with forty cases of heatstroke on board; existence in a small cruiser surrounded by steel plating in this climate would seem a test even for the British tar.

All the way to Busrah we had passed a string of hospital ships bound for India, a testimony to the truth of what they had told us in Bombay. On the evening of July 30th we arrived at the Shatt-el-Arab lightship, and anchored outside the bar for the night. The sea here is very shallow, being only three fathoms in depth, and the land at the mouth so low-lying as to be practically out of sight from the bar. Here in 1914 General Delamain, with a brigade of troops, made his landing at Fao, and captured the fort after its guns had been silenced by our warships. The Shatt-el-Arab (Arab river) is the estuary formed by the junction of the Tigris and Euphrates about a hundred miles from the sea. Next morning we crossed the bar and entered the river; it reminds one of the Nile with the date palms on either hand and white desert beyond. The *shamal*, a red-hot wind with driving sand, made one seek protection; it blows for six weeks, and is regarded as a welcome relief in the long monotony of the hot weather, sometimes a questionable point; the still heat of an oven or a fiery blast and driving sand!

Abadan, once a considerable port on the sea coast, now about forty miles upriver, was almost invisible in the fog of sand and scorching wind. Here were the dockyard for the river gunboats and the terminus of the hundred-mile pipe line between the oilfields and the refineries of the Anglo-Persian Oil Company. Just above Abadan the channel was blocked by three vessels sunk in the fairway by the Turks, leaving, however, a narrow channel close in to the right bank. At three o'clock that afternoon we came to the end of our voyage, Busrah, the base and G.H.Q. of Indian Expeditionary Force "D."

After the Moslem invasion in the seventh century, a new city called Al-Busrah, said to mean "the black pebbles," was built some miles inland from the Sassanian city Ubullah on the feverish estuary; the former, however, has passed with the ages, and the modern Busrah occupies the site of the ancient Ubullah.

As soon as war broke out in Europe the authorities in Constantinople sent secret telegrams to the Nationalist faction in Busrah to enlist feeling against the Allies. On the arrival of the British expedition in November, 1914, many of the Arabs joined the Turks in the natural desire to defend their homes and incited further by lure of loot and other Ottoman promises. Fortunately the British advance was rapid, or the whole country might have been enlisted against us. Busrah was captured on November 22nd, after some hard fighting.

The place is famous at least for its climate; the humid heat hangs heavy on the lungs, everything is saturated, ink runs on the paper, and matches will barely strike. Endure the day, but the night brings no relief. There is no freshness in a Busrah summer, and the ravages of prickly heat, mosquito, and sand-fly combine to shrivel all impulse and desire. The town and its surroundings are intersected by canals and lagoons, and densely sown with date palms, their "feet in water and their heads in Hell," as the Arab saying goes. Busrah city itself is some way up a creek, its suburb on the banks being called Ashar.

The inhabitants are a cosmopolitan crowd: Baghdadi Jews, Greeks, Swahilis, Lurs, Bakhtiaris, Abyssinians, Chaldeans, Zanzibaris, Armenians, Persians, Kurds, Indians, and Arabs, jostle each other in the bazaars. In the stream were rows of *dhows* from Indian, African, Persian and Arabian ports; a great date trade has been carried on for centuries. Time does not seem to have changed either the trade or the ships and their crews. There they lay as of old, with their graceful lines and carved woodwork; the Arab captain and his friends decorously drinking coffee in the stern, and the negro crew, sons of the slave trade, bickering in the bow; Vasco da Gama would have seen no change. In utter contrast to this were the six huge masts of the high-powered wireless station crackling out forty words a minute to the other side of the world.

As at Venice, the means of progression at Busrah is by water; instead of the gondola there is the *bellum*, a long canoe strongly made and easily capsized. One goes to the bazaar up the Ashar Creek, past rows of Arab cafes and dancing saloons. On the west side of the harbour were the merchants' warehouses, stores, offices, and landing stages. Many of these buildings had been appropriated for the accommodation of G.H.Q. and hospitals. On the other side were the old Turkish barracks, flying the White Ensign, used as a depot by the Royal Navy, but soon evacuated except for storage purposes on account of disease. The harbour was busy with small craft such as motor-launches, *dhows*, smart Navy boats, tugs, *bellums*, and *gufas*, the latter circular coracles made of tarred mud and matting, and unchanged since the days of the Bible. A curious medley of all ages and all races!

On either bank, as far as the eye could see, the long, lean palm trees swayed in the hot wind; outside the white desert blazed to the horizon.

My first day on shore I had an interview with General Sir Percy Lake, and was generally busy learning the situation. The staff at G.H.Q. looked tired and washed out, the result of long office hours in the Busrah hot weather.

The strength of the R.F.C. at this time in Mesopotamia was one skeleton squadron at the Front, and an Aircraft Park at the base. There was also a Kite Balloon section of the R.N.A.S. under Commander Wrottesly, R.N.

As will be remembered, Kut had fallen on April 23rd of this year, in spite of the indescribable valour and devotion of the relieving force, who, in the face of overwhelming difficulties, had again and again striven to break through. There had been no time to lose, and brigades straight off the sea from France were rushed in and decimated as soon as they arrived. The enemy still held the same position at Sannayat on the left bank in which he had withstood our attacks in April. His line was flanked on the one side by the Suwaikieh Marsh, and on the other by the river, whose bank from Sannayat to Kut was also entrenched. On the right bank of the Tigris it extended from a point three miles N.E. of Kut in a S.W. direction to the river Hai, two miles below its junction with the Tigris, and thence across the Hai to the N.W. The line of the Hai was occupied for several miles with posts and mounted Arab auxiliaries.

On the left bank of the Tigris our trenches were within a hundred and twenty yards of the Turkish front line; on the right bank our troops were established eleven miles upstream of Sannayat, with outposts about two miles from those of the Turk. In these positions desultory warfare, with intermittent artillery and aerial activity, was carried on. An Indian Division occupied

Nasiriyeh on the Euphrates, where the surrounding tribesmen were mostly hostile; further up that river, where Turkish influence was rife, there was a small enemy force. Railway construction had already been commenced towards Nasiriyeh.

The Aircraft Park, at Tanooma, on the other side of Busrah Harbour, was a collection of palm-leaf huts with a few iron-roofed brick sheds, surrounded by desert. Here such arrears of work had accumulated that it was hard to know where to begin, and the men who were left had little life in them. It was only possible to work in the hours of dawn, for by nine o'clock the sun was getting up, and any remaining energy was necessary for bare existence. A large percentage of our staff were sick, the hospitals were overflowing, and very few reinforcements arriving in the country ever reached their units, but went sick at Busrah, taking up valuable room in hospital that was needed for men evacuated from the front.

Lack of labour was seriously holding up the unlading of stores urgently required by the force up river; coolies were few and difficult, and troops were not to be spared from drafts for the fighting forces, fifty *per cent*, of whom had gone sick. The congestion of shipping in Busrah harbour, as a result of this, was serious at a time when all the Empire's resources in tonnage were necessary to fight the submarine menace. Some ships had been lying in harbour for months, and it was said that others had returned to India, having only cleared a portion of their cargo in order not to waste time when there was any space available. Nine new aeroplanes which had been waiting a month to be unloaded were not got ashore till several weeks later. The base at Busrah seemed to be congested with stores of every description, yet owing to lack of labour and shallow draft river transport, the fighting force were hard pressed to maintain themselves.

Next morning, August 4th, we started up river in the steamer T3, attached to the Royal Flying Corps; the landscape consists of grass and scrub dotted with Arab villages, dead flat to the horizon, and rather like the White Nile.

The waters of the Euphrates flow into the Tigris at two places. The swamps and lakes away to the West, in which various channels of the Euphrates lose themselves, drain into a common stream which empties itself at Gurmat Ali, about five miles above Busrah. Kurnah, another forty miles on, is the junction of the Tigris and the only navigable Euphrates channel. On the spit of land formed by the two rivers is the reputed site of the Garden of Eden; the stranger is still shown the Tree of Knowledge by the Arabs. The two streams flowing along side by side are quite distinct before they merge, the muddy white of the Tigris on the one hand and the clear blue of the Euphrates on the other. In the Middle Ages the Tigris, after reaching Kut, changed from its original and modern course, and flowed south down what is now the Shatt-el-Hai, losing itself as that river does in the swamps. It is uncertain when the river changed back into its present course, but Ralph Fitch and John Newberie, two Englishmen who had come to Baghdad down the Euphrates in 1583, reached Busrah by boat, passing Kurnah, *a castle which standeth upon the point where the river Furro* (Euphrates) *and the river of Bagdet* (Tigris) *doe meet.*" These Englishmen eventually reached the court of Akbar, the Great Moghul, where they separated; Newberie was murdered in the Punjab, Fitch, after many vicissitudes, returned up the Tigris in 1588, and succeeded in regaining England. It is impossible to imagine the hardships which these early pioneers must have endured.

There are no crocodiles in these rivers, but their place is taken by sharks, and tortoises are to be seen swimming in hundreds; the bird life of the whole country is wonderful.

In the evening we passed Ezra's tomb: a blue-domed building and haunt of pilgrims in time of peace. Records as far back as the tenth century A.D. speak of this place as renowned through the country as a spot where prayers were answered. We anchored for the night in midstream, for in those days it was unsafe to tie up to the bank. Jackals howled one to sleep. The following afternoon we crawled into Amara against a *shamal* gale that burnt the eyes in their sockets. Lieutenant Kelly, in charge of the R.F.C. advanced store depot, met us here, and we groped ashore to have a look at the place and inspect the mule transport fitting out for the front; the wheels of the carts had all shrunk away from their tyres.

Amara is a large town, consisting of the regulation Arab houses of mud bricks, which reach to the river on either side; the two banks were connected by a bridge of boats left behind by the Turks. The bazaar is famed for its silver-work from Damascus to Peshawur, and is thronged by Jews, Chaldeans, Arabs, Persians, Kurds, and Indians. The place must have been infested with spies. There were two miles of hospital camps, and most of the available buildings had been converted into hospitals; hospital tents even surrounded the gallows in the square. One of the Arab houses on the river had been turned into an officers' club, and here it was possible to get a cool whiskey-and-soda on the veranda of an evening. Amara had been captured on June 3rd, 1915, by twenty-two sailors and soldiers who sailed up the river in a shallow-draught gunboat and demanded the surrender of the town with its garrison of seven hundred Turks. An audacious stroke of successful bluff, as the Norfolk Regiment did not arrive till the next day.

The day after leaving Amara we grounded on a mud bank at 6 a.m. The Arab crew and pilot were useless, but we managed to kedge her off ourselves after three hours, only to go aground again an hour later. In spite of many more arduous hours spent in the heat and wind, we failed to find a channel, merely moving from one shoal to another; but at last, after dark, another steamer came downstream and hauled us into deeper water by a heavy wire. She had been on the mud herself for ten hours. The river was at its lowest and the channels continually altering; we were told that with our four feet three inches draught it was doubtful whether we should get above Ali-Gharbi, twenty-five miles short of our destination, Sheikh Saad. The heat during the whole of the journey upstream had been terrific; the two batmen who had started with us were both down, one with dysentery, the other with stroke. One's apparel consisted of shorts, shirt sleeves and a *topi*, without shoes or stockings. In the evening one was

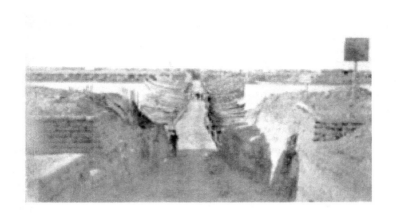

BOAT BRIDGE SHEIKH SAAD

SHEIKH SAAD

glad to hang over the side of the ship on a rope and be towed slowly through the water, which, though thick and nasty to taste, was at least cool.

Ali-Gharbi proved a mere collection of Arab shelters and the tents of a small British post; not a tree to be seen. Here we left T3, as she would only have blown on the shoals in the shallow and tortuous channels above. I shall never forget going ashore that morning in this god-forgotten spot; bending low against the gale, I searched for a British officer. Eventually there appeared a ragged individual in pyjamas and helmet; he had been there all summer and had long since lost all interest in life. The arrival of fresh blood from England, however, cheered him, and talk of London over a bottle of warm beer seemed to awaken further desire to live.

Our intention of crossing the desert to Sheikh Saad in a motor was not advised on account of possible attack by Arabs, so a telegram was sent to squadron H.Q. for their motor-boat. Captain Murray, commanding at the time, met us, and we ran up to Sheikh Saad in four hours in spite of taking several shoals at twelve knots.

The tents of a squadron of Flying Corps and a few other troops were the sole means of distinguishing Sheikh Saad from Ali-Gharbi; otherwise, as spake the British Tommy, *there was miles and miles and miles of sweet damn all!*

CHAPTER 2

A Land of Sand, Sun and Sorrow

And that Inverted Bowl we call The Sky,
Whereunder crawling coop't we live and die,
Lift not thy hand to IT for help—for IT
Rolls impotently on as Thou or I.
　　　　　—Omar.

The enemy's aerodrome was at Shumran, a few miles above Kut, his flying unit being manned by Germans and equipped with Fokker and Albatross machines. Hitherto their sky had been clear; with only an occasional old B.E., Henry Farman, or Voisin to hinder them, their morale was excellent. To quote Sir Percy Lake's despatch:

"As regards aviation, the superiority of certain of the enemy planes over any of our machines in the matter of speed, combined with a large reduction in the number of our pilots (due to sickness partly attributable to overwork), enabled the enemy in May and June to establish what was very nearly a mastery of the air."

It was essential to destroy that morale, as in order to fulfil the role of close co-operation with cavalry, artillery, and infantry, and carry on the photography and mapping of any area in the hands of the enemy, an Air Service must be in moral supremacy. The personnel of the squadron were severity under strength and most of them sick men, unable to leave their tents many days of the week. More machines were, however, got into commission, and would go out in the early "hours of the morning hunting for Huns. The effort was not in vain, and within a week Lieutenants Lander and Barr shot down a Fokker that had come up from the Shumran aerodrome, and been previously engaged by another B.E., in which action Lieutenant Hon. J. Rodney was wounded. After this, aerial combats were intermittent, and the enemy seemed to lose appetite for close action.

There was yet another way to shake his morale; and with bombing raids he was harried in his lair by day or night.

On the night of the 14th three of us opened the ball: time was allowed for the Turk to have his supper and get to sleep; he had never been bombed by night before, and we hoped that the surprise of this little jaunt might further its effect. Just after eleven Captain de Havilland left the ground with a cheery wave and was gone in the darkness; a few minutes later came "Contact, sir!" from my mechanic, and I was away.

Our course took us over the desert west of the river, which shone like quicksilver in the moonlight far to starboard. A strong head-wind made progress slow, but it was pleasant to be up in the cool vastness of the night above that strange country. It seemed ever so long ago that I had left England. A series of flashes in the distance ahead dispelled reverie; D. H. was attacking. Gliding slowly with engine off, I arrived short of the aerodrome at a height of 400 feet, when suddenly there burst a storm of heavy and concentrated rifle fire from what must have been at least a thousand rifles under well-directed control. It had been my lot during the war to come under fusillades of varying intensity, but this reception was perhaps the warmest up to date: the sound was like the tearing of a piece of calico. After dropping the bombs on the hangars my speed downwind gave the Turks small chance. Captain Herring, who had followed me, came in for a similar reception, but D. H. had surprised them as had been expected. The results were unknown in the uncertain light and dust of the explosions; time would tell.

The evening's airing finished with a cheery supper by the Tigris at 2 a.m. off sardines and coffee with the lads who could not sleep for sand flies. The sand flies at Sheikh Saad defied description, and mosquito nets were of no avail, the net specially designed against these pests entailing a mesh so small as to make ventilation impossible; the expedient of emptying the kerosene from one's *butti* (lamp) over bed and body gave relief for perhaps an hour till it had dried off, and the torture started again. In those days men sold their souls for kerosene. There is a place called Bor, a thousand miles up the White Nile; those who have been there and sampled its mosquitoes will realise what were the sand flies at Sheikh Saad. They came with a roar at sundown, sleep was out of the question. During the night desperate humans would be seen walking about the camp smoking cigarettes; to help the night through, "*chota* pegs" and sandwiches would be laid out under the moon. In spite of all this we were a cheery crowd.

There was "Bert"—sometime cavalry officer—planter in Burma—artillery brigade commander in South Africa; now hawk-like observer—mess president and cocktail-mixer- in-chief; there was little that "Bert" did not know or could not do; his joy and the youthfulness of his heart were those of a boy, his manner that of a courtier. "Bert" became famous through the land.

Then "D. H.," otherwise "Mark 2," being the youngest of a famous pair. Life was not serious for "D. H." The ground hardly knew him, but when it did it smiled; he feared neither God nor Man. His mate was "Oo-Er," a vermilion machine and the terror of the Turk. When by chance on the ground, he would play golf round the aerodrome, a palpitating tyke following in his train.

In the dog days came "Chocolo," which is short for "Chocololovitch" (after a soldier comedian who sang a song of that name), a broth of a boy with a brogue of Fermanagh. He presented himself from his Indian unit at a time when there was no vacancy for embryo observers; however, as a result of the difficulties of transport for his return and a determination not to budge, "Chocolo "remained for two years.

Then there was "Bobby," an imperturbable representative from Caledonia. Bobby was stolid; when threatened with expulsion after appalling crashes, he would remain quite stoically undisturbed with a grin on his face. He said little. The only times that Bobby blossomed to the outside world were on such occasions as New Year's Eve or St. Andrew's Night, when our friend would become suddenly brilliant, the central figure of the evening; after which he would retire into his quiet canny shell until another Festival came round on which he thought it fit to blossom forth once more. Later on he distinguished himself by shooting down a Hun in aerial combat and received the Military Cross. Questioned by the G.O.C. as to how many he had crashed, Bobby replied: "Sixteen; fifteen English and one German, sir." His next crash, alas! was his last.

"Anzac," transferred to us from the Remounts; his youth had been spent astride of a horse in the back-blocks of Queensland; the early days of the war saw him a trooper in the Bombay Light Horse. He would amuse us with yarns of his charging troop on the sands at Colaba, and how, when they had run away, he wheeled them into the sea. A great-hearted Australian, Anzac had never been to Europe. We shall meet more of this gallant company later; to describe them all would require a separate volume.

This period of the campaign was stagnant as regards the land force; sullen trench warfare on the left bank and an affair of outposts on the right. The Arabs were a continual source of worry; in fact the war was one of British against Turk, the whole surrounded by Arabs. They were like jackals hanging about both camps, and woe betide the Englishman or Turk who was caught alone. All our camps had to be fortified, wired in, and defended, for the marauders were out on a foray every night. The cunning and skill of the Pathan on the North-West Frontier were nothing compared with that of the Bedouin. Somehow he would get through the wire and sentries and make away with a rifle from under a sleeper's pillow without awakening him; it seemed supernatural. The wire was thickened, grenades ready to detonate were hung upon it, and yet these Arab thieves would be in the camp by bright moonlight carrying off arms and ammunition. If alarmed they would not hesitate to plunge in their long knives, and several good lives were lost in this fashion. Most of us slept with loaded revolvers in our hands; this made movement about the camp somewhat precarious by night, and walking down a row of tents one would hear "click, click, click," the wakeful sleepers cocking their guns! Occasionally someone would blaze off at a shadow in the middle of the stillness; one night a poor donkey who had strayed too far took two holes in his belly as a result.

The Arabs on the Hai river, a thickly populated district, were in sympathy with the Turks and a nasty thorn on our left flank. Not far from Sheikh Saad was Gussab's Fort, a hotbed of these marauders. We bombed it most mornings, and after several direct hits its occupants retired into the various villages of the district. These Bedouins were all armed and well mounted, and when organised proved a formidable foe. A savage, cunning folk, they would dig up the dead to get the blankets; torture and mutilation were regular practices, withal they were brave men.

It was my fortune once to witness from the air a battle of one tribe against another to the north of the Suwaikieh Marsh, a sideshow quite apart from the Turks or British. But it was an Englishman who led one side, one Englishman alone leading a wild savage tribe into fierce battle against Turkish friendlies on our right flank. The career of this Englishman may never be written, yet in the history of the world there is probably no romance that can equal it; most people have heard, and much has worthily been sung, of Colonel Lawrence, of Syrian and Hedjaz fame; the story of Colonel Leachman is perhaps even stranger. Before the war Leachman spent his time wandering over large tracts of Arabia, and when British forces went to Mesopotamia he was employed politically in the desert. His prestige was amazing, and his name known to every Bedouin from Aden to Mosul. He lived in that desert from January to December dressed as an Arab, and with his boy Hussein wandered about amongst the tribes, perhaps even behind the Turks, organising, compelling, acquiring priceless information. There was a price on his head, and he lived with his life in his hands, but he could shoot a tribesman dead for misdeeds in front of the tribe and no hand would be lifted against him. Occasional visits to G.H.Q., and he would be gone, riding out to the horizon on his little Arab pony with his long legs dangling nearly to the ground. Eventually he would return wizened and thin, with probably a severe dose of fever after months in the desert in the heat of the summer, living on Arab food and water. Throughout Eastern Arabia the people were under the impression that it was Leachman who commanded the British forces, and even that he was the King of England. On special cards that were printed for flying officers, to produce in the event of coming down in the desert, was written his name in large Arabic letters. Such was the magic of his personality. When I left Mesopotamia two years later, I had not seen Leachman for several months; he was still in the desert.

The days at Sheikh Saad were a heavy strain on both health and nerves, the former, I suppose, being the cause of the latter. Our camp was situated on the river bank between two hospitals, the one downstream being the cholera hospital; a mournful procession of funerals at nightfall does not tend to elevate the spirits of a fever-eaten community. There was no fresh food, and a scale of only half rations; the bully-beef was liquid in its tin, and had to be poured out. The only cool drink in the 24 hours was the water in a *chatti*, hung up to a tent rope overnight and drunk before the sun got up. The porous earthenware jar causes evaporation, thereby cooling the contents, providing there is no sun. In the day all liquid was hot, the glasses got almost too hot to hold. Tinned fruit was issued in an effort to combat the scurvy, but was found of little avail; scurvy and jaundice were very rife. As usual, the British troops withstood the climate and trying conditions far better than the Indians, who went down like flies. The war was one of blockade, and the resultant inactivity of an army employed only in fighting sand and sun was a factor to increase sickness. When "Turk" was added to these adversaries the effect was contrary, spirits improved and with them health. Inactivity induces disease.

The R.F.C. were lucky in being under "double-fly" tents; most of the army had to sit in their helmets under single-fly 80-lb. shelters through which the sun's rays streamed, making the temperature intolerable. Even within our own tents the thermometer sometimes stood well over 130 deg. Fahr. during the day. With the ceasing of the jackals' howls the dawn would come and reveal for a few minutes the Pusht-i-Kuh away to the East in Persia; to the rest of the horizon there was limitless desert. How we used to hate watching the sun's rays shoot up from behind these hills, then the old red ball would top the summits and all animal life would seek cover.

Horizons vanished, the sky became steel coloured, another day had started to take its toll. About nine o'clock, with a few heralding puffs and "sand devils," the *shamal* would be down, driving the sand five or six thousand feet high till nightfall; then the imagination would stray to green fields of England or soft Highland rain. We at least thanked our stars that our lot did not take us to the trenches at Sannayat; as usual throughout the war the "enduring" was done by the infantry.

The sand-grouse were a great feature at Sheikh Saad; they were there during the summer in tens of thousands. What might be taken for a distant black cloud in the early morning would be a flock of these birds congregating at the river to drink. One soon learnt their regular flights, and three guns and two loaders would have been welcome, for they streamed over unceasingly. Most of us had guns, but cartridges were at a premium. When there were enough one could take the sporting shots, rocketers at any angle; but if, as often happened, only a dozen cartridges remained in the camp they would be handed over to an expert in order that he might secure the only available form of fresh meat for the mess by fair means or foul. On such occasions Paddy Maguire would be sent out and watched intently from a distance stalking the unsuspecting birds with artful cunning. He would wait till he got three or four in line on the ground, and then, with an ancient *bundook* that he had brought from Co. Clare, rake them with deadly effect. With a fresh consignment of cartridges three or four guns would go out and have splendid shooting, bringing back enough to feed the whole squadron, a welcome change for the men from the everlasting tinned food. In winter the sand-grouse disappeared.

We had both land and water transport at this stage of the campaign. On the river there were 100-ft. barges divided into the workshops, darkrooms, stores, etc., essential to a flying unit. These barges remained or moved with their flights, for it was a river war, and the Tigris being the only artery of supply and communication the force could not move far from it. Plying between Busrah and the front we had further barges towed by two allotted steamers, the T3, a river boat from India, and the *Bahmanshir*, once the yacht of the Sheikh of Mohammerah. The T3 drew too much water, and she spent many weary hours aground; later on this stopped her working entirely in the higher reaches during the low water season. The *Bahmanshir* was early Victorian, and her bed-plate in the engine-room being cracked she could never steam more than half speed; the engine was held in place by the main steam-pipe! Despite this the *Bahmanshir*, with her enterprising Arab skipper and Dago engineer, did many a rapid scramble over the shoals twix't base and front, making up in navigation for what she lacked in power.

At Sheikh Saad there was also a *mahala*, a craft similar to the *dahabeah* of the Nile, used for the storage of petrol and bombs. The Arab skipper of this *mahala* came one day to my office tent. I heard someone hovering about outside, arid calling out to ask who it was received the reply, "I the *mahala-walla*-captain-*sahib*, my lighter is sinking" (he always referred to his craft as his "lighter"), and there was the ruffian beaming from ear to ear very pleased with his effort at English. He was a genial, friendly soul and full of the high office he held with the British Army. Having evidently become tired of Sheikh Saad, and desiring to return to his wives and the flesh pots of Busrah, he had made a hole in the bottom of his vessel, which was leaking badly and afforded good excuse to retire to dock; he also asked for his wages; the inference was obvious. However, his "lighter" was an unnecessary luxury, so I made no demur, and after great ceremonial and assurances of immediate return to help us win the war, he and his chattering crew sailed away.

For land transport we possessed three light lorries, a Hupmobile car, and fifty-six Australian mules to haul six specially-constructed wagons. This mule transport was the great pride of the R.F.C., the personnel were Australians assisted by Madrassi boys, and "Anzac" was in charge. It was a well-trained unit; eight 16-hand mules would move a wagon across country at rattling speed. For exercise in the evenings we would harness ten or twelve pair to a wagon and manoeuvre about at a canter.

It must be remembered that there were no roads, so that the motor transport had to rely on picking its way across the desert. A narrow-gauge railway was built from Sheikh Saad out to Sinn, the divisional H.Q. on the right bank, all the material having been shipped from India to Busrah and up the Tigris in barges. This railway, twenty miles in length, was protected along its southern and exposed side by a chain of blockhouses connected by barbed wire; to the North flowed the river. Sheikh Saad became the advanced base for the force.

In August the Sannayat position was garrisoned by the 7th and the right bank by the 3rd Indian Divisions. Tigris Corps H.Q. were close behind Sannayat, but on the opposite side of the river; in fact, Corps H.Q. were only 4,000 yards from the Turkish front line. The Turks might have shelled the camp any day, but they apparently were anxious to *let sleeping dogs lie.*

The 13th Division, the only British Division in the Force, came back to Sheikh Saad and marched on south to Amara to train and reduce the ration strength at the front. Earlier in the year this Division, from Gallipoli, and the 3rd and 7th Indian Divisions, from France, had arrived to be plunged straight into the desperate fighting for the relief of Kut. Nasiriyeh, on the Euphrates, and its L. of C. were garrisoned by the 15th Indian Division.

The dispositions at the end of August were thus:—

Tigris Corps—Lieutenant -General A. S. Cobbe, V.C.
3rd Division—Major-General H. D'U. Keary.

British Position on the Tigris from May to December 13th 1916

7th Division—Brig. -General C. E. Norie.

13th Division—Major-General W. Cayley, at Amara.

14th Division—Major-General R. G. Egerton.

15th Division Major-General H. T. Brooking, at Nasiriyeh.

Lieutenant-General F. S. Maude succeeded Lieutenant- General Sir Percy Lake as G.O.C.-in-C. on the latter being invalided.

Forward landing grounds were made at Corps H.Q. at Dujailah (14th Division), and at Arab Village (7th Division) to aid co-operation. The strategic situation was a curious one, and to our advantage; the enemy's communications on the left bank were prolonged and exposed to our force situated on the right bank. The Suwaikieh Marsh protected the northern flank of our Sannayat position, and our troops were so disposed on the right bank to prevent any attempt on our left flank, a movement which would have meant long and hazardous marches for the enemy. During August a flight of two Voisins and two Henry Farman machines was sent to Arab Village to co-operate with the artillery of the 7th Division. It was not practicable to detail a flight for Dujailah for co-operation with the 14th Division, as Corps H.Q. pointed out to me the difficulty of feeding the force already there without being further burdened. Dujailah was a two days' journey across the desert.

Wireless gear was fitted in all machines, and artillery co-operation practised and developed. By the end of August the work of registration of the enemy positions was in full swing. Great difficulties had been experienced by the force due to the complete lack of reliable maps. The only method of mapping a hostile country is by photography, and an extensive programme in this respect was carried out each morning, commencing with an area of forty square miles round Kut. A close reconnaissance of the whole front was maintained daily, and distant reconnaissances were frequently sent to Hai-Town (Kut-el-Hai), Azizieh, and Mendali, the latter being an undertaking of two hundred miles across waterless desert with a complete lack of landmarks, no mean performance with the old B.E. aeroplane.

We did not know what Simla or the War Office intended as regards the Mesopotamian campaign; some thought that we should merely hold the enemy's forces where we were, but the most prevalent idea was that we should capture Kut in the cold weather and wipe out the stain of its loss; some even thought that we might evacuate our present positions and take up a defensive line somewhere down river. How little we guessed the great events that were in store!

A system of Emergency calls from all wireless stations and "Clear line" telephone calls was established to signal the locality of enemy aircraft as soon as sighted. While the weather was still hot aerial work during the day was limited to the early hours, for the late afternoon was as hot as midday till the sun went down; then it was dark. Cooler air was not to be found under an altitude of 3,000 feet, and little difference could be felt much under 5,000 feet. Flying in the night one would start in fairly cool atmosphere, but on reaching 500 feet one entered the hot air of the day. It was a curious phenomenon; the belt of hot air on the ground during the day rose up at night, being lighter than the air cooled by the radiation of the earth. Flying in the hot weather was a great strain, and, after service in France, it was odd to see a pilot going off for a long flight dressed only in shorts, stockings, and shirt, with a helmet bound down on to his head, for at 5,000 feet the sun's rays are as fierce as on the ground.

An attack of fever stretched me out at the end of August, and I was laid up in hospital in an Arab house on the banks of the river at Amara. It was in the days before fans and when the supply of ice was limited; the wards were crowded and the sand-flies at night intolerable; however, it was active service in an uncivilised land, and the nurses were all Florence Nightingales. We lay and sweated and shivered, drank tinned milk and water, cursed the orderly because the soda-water was hot and Fate had sent us to Mesopotamia. Then we staggered out on to the veranda of the officers' club and built up strength to go down river to India or back to the front.

A large percentage were wont to get clear of the country if they could; it was only human nature, and others like myself, in fat jobs or on the gilded staff, could hardly blame the point of view of the poor infantry subaltern who, shaken by fever and dysentery after a miserable existence through the summer, was tempted by the thought of embarking in a nice white hospital ship for other climes and seeing the last of this fire country. For the Great Cause, however, it was necessary to stop the tremendous wastage caused by the wholesale evacuation of personnel.

Once sick, there was little difficulty for those who meant to, in getting out of the country, and it had become rather a disease. General Maude took the matter seriously in hand; convalescent camps were developed, and any case of evacuation had to be approved by high authority. The effect was satisfactory, and many more patients were brought back to health and duty without leaving the country.

A large Sheikh's palace, named Beit Naama, situated on the banks of the river about five miles downstream from Busrah, served well as an officers' convalescent hospital. It was splendidly fitted up, and became a popular institution under its sporting O.C., Major Munro. He added attractions to the place till it rivalled Harrogate or Strathpeffer: fishing, boating on the river, a small desert golf course, concerts in the evening, and comfortable quarters were all inducements to health.

By September the nights were cooler, and the day temperature seldom went above 110 Fahr. With this change scope expanded and style was less cramped. Aeroplane reconnaissance showed considerable work being carried out by the Turks on two jetties at the mouth of the Hai River. It was thought that the enemy might possibly be building these jetties as a means of diverting some of the water of the Tigris down the Shatt-el-Hai. At the time there was only just sufficient water in the Tigris to bring the river craft up, and had the Turk succeeded in such an operation the effect might have been disastrous. We kept a careful watch on the place, which was examined and photographed daily. Fortunately our fears were groundless, and later inspection of the site proved the enormous difficulties in the way of such an undertaking.

In the first week of September, Brigadier-General W. Salmond, R.F.C., arrived in the country and spent three days at Sheikh Saad inspecting and advising. For the supply of personnel, special stores, and certain administrative purposes, the R.F.C in Mesopotamia had come under and formed part of the new Middle East Brigade, commanded by General Salmond, which included the units in Egypt, Salonika, Palestine (later), Mesopotamia, and East Africa. Major MacEwen, at the base with the title of Assistant-Director of Aeronautics, was in direct touch by cable with H.Q. Middle East in Cairo, the Air Board in London, and the Port Detachment in Bombay.

The spoke of communication led direct to the hub, there was no need to delay or refer to others, we could act at once; the process was invaluable. Throughout September, reconnaissance, photography, and artillery co-operation kept all available machines busy each day. A web of intelligence was being woven and added to that gathered by other means at Tigris Corps H.Q. In a desert country with efficient aerial observation it is impossible for an enemy to alter his dispositions without discovery; the movement of a few tents or shelters can be spotted at once, and there are no woods or buildings in which to hide his men.

The following specimen of a reconnaissance report as telegraphed daily to Corps H.Q. may be of interest:

23/9/1916.
Reconnaissance 6.30 to 8 a.m. reports: At Shumran aerodrome two machines on ground. One hangar damaged. Jetties opposite Hai mouth are joined completely into continuous dam from Tigris right bank to sand bank in midstream. No sign of work on channel North of sand bank. Suwada camp area unchanged, camps being similar in pitching and number of tents to these prior to yesterday. Shumran camp area left bank unchanged. Kut camp area forty tents at 35 B 7/7 reduced to ten and fifty at 36 C 2/8 reduced to twenty-five. Narwhan area unchanged.

Shumran right bank area thirty tents at 35 C 0/4. Hai bridge area camps as follows: forty tents at 36 B 3/2, ten at 36 C 2/3, ten at 35 D 9/1, forty and transport animals or horses at 46 B 3/5. Total, hundred tents; fifty empty pontoons along right bank at 35 B 42; six laden pontoons floating downstream just west of TC 41. Shipping—three steamers, three barges, three *mahelas*. At Narwhan N.W. gun position is occupied. West position is covered oven East position is empty. New gun position at 16 A 5/6; two pits containing tents and two empty; two or three pits occupied B 17. No indication of any considerable withdrawal of troops or alterations in dispositions.

The Arabs on our flanks were also closely watched, and any threatening concentration dealt with by bomb and machine-gun fire. These attacks had great moral effect, and often caused the tribesmen to strike their tents and leave the district altogether. Raids continued on the Shumran aerodrome, and Turkish deserters reported that it came as a great surprise to them that machines could fly by night, and that much consternation was caused thereby. The enemy made "dug-out" hangars for his machines, and placed dummy aeroplanes on his aerodrome. He also organised a system of flares along all routes of possible approach by our aeroplanes. These flares would be lit as we passed, and so give warning to the next station ahead, till his aerodrome took up the tale and could prepare accordingly. It was not encouraging to the pilot to watch these flares as he continued on his way, and wondered what sort of reception was in store for him.

I think the most notable of these expeditions was that by Lieutenant Hon. J. S. Rodney and Second-Lieutenant J. S. Windsor, who arrived at the Turkish aerodrome at dawn on September 23rd, and dropped their bombs from a height of under 100 feet. Lieutenant Rodney's attack was practically a surprise, and he met with little opposition. Second-Lieutenant Windsor had drawn the second place and started ten minutes later; the enemy were waiting for him. With a splendid dash he went right down from the mirk of the dawn into a tornado of rifle and machine-gun fire, placed his bombs with accuracy, and got away. It was a glorious bit of cutting-out work, and on the slow old B.E. the odds against him were very great.

As a result of this raid, one enemy aeroplane was destroyed and one badly damaged. Both these officers received the Military Cross it seems sad that this decoration was so often given during the war for mere clerical work far removed from the field of battle, and entailing no danger whatever; after all, there is little more the individual can do than offer his life the reward for those who do it should surely be kept exclusive.

Co-operation with the artillery on both sides of the Tigris entailed heavy work. Including the registration of enemy positions, a systematic programme for the destruction of enemy gun-pits behind Sannayat was begun, and, as the outcome of the keenness and friendly relations between the Artillery and the Air, the results gradually became somewhat destructive to the Turk. Ammunition dumps were blown up, and Turkish guns received direct hits more often than they could afford. On the morning of the 23rd, while Captains Herring and King-Harman were spotting for the guns, they observed the "enemy aircraft" signal at one of the ground stations; immediately shaping course in their old "Voisin," they five minutes later picked up a suspicious looking machine at about 6,000 feet.

In turning to get between them and the sun it showed up the black crosses clearly, and the two machines passed left hand to left hand about 150 yards apart. The enemy could walk round the Voisin, and, with rudder control shot away, the British machine went down in a spinning nose dive amid a hail of bullets from the Hun. With great coolness Herring pulled her out when near the ground, and only crashed his under-carriage. Herring and King-Harman got back to Arab Village, took up a Henry Farman, and, directing the fire, obliterated the target from which they had been interrupted. Alas! King-Harman met his end in a crash with Lieutenant Hayward a few weeks later.

At the end of September it was necessary for me to journey to Nasiriyeh to arrange regarding the despatch of an R.F.C. detachment. I started down the river for Busrah in a steamer full of Indian sick; there was even less depth in the thick grey trickle than on the journey up, and many hours were spent on the mud. On these journeys one had to take one's own food, and my boy "Charlie" was almost a wizard in the way he would produce a three-course dinner out of practically nothing at all, at any time or place.

After a day at Busrah, and an interview with General Maude, MacEwen and I left the ground early one morning to fly to Nasiriyeh. The whole way we were passing over swamps and lakes. Above the Hamar Lake the water stretched to the horizon and we seemed to be crossing the sea; this water coming from the Shatt-el-Hai and Euphrates drains into the Tigris by the channels at Gurmat-Ali and Kurnah. The land, as far as the eye can see, is intersected by canals, covered with vegetation, and thickly populated; a very different country from the Tigris. The Arabs were hostile, and, apart from the impossibility of effecting a landing anywhere, it would have been a sorry affair to have had to come down. Sometime before two flying officers while crossing this country had made a forced landing, and been murdered. We spent the day with General Brooking, and made arrangements for a detachment of two machines, with wireless and photography equipment, to join him.

Nasiriyeh was like a garden after Sheikh Saad, and the force stationed there lived on the fat of the land, with fresh meat, vegetables, and fruit. The fish supply also was abundant, being a regular trade of the inhabitants of the town. The British troops had just returned from battle, six miles to the North-East, having routed five thousand Arabs, whose losses were 436 killed and some 800 wounded.

It struck one on arriving at Nasiriyeh that the place was in a state of siege; the town was surrounded by defences, outside of which it was dangerous to proceed unless with strong escort; the means of egress and ingress with Busrah being by river convoy. These convoys, after leaving Kurnah, proceeded by the Euphrates channel as far as the Hamar Lake; here the water was only one or two feet deep, and men, guns, baggage, and stores were transferred into *bellums*. Two or three days were then spent sitting cramped in these craft under the fierce sun, poling and paddling along out of sight of land.

Eventually another Euphrates channel was reached where one of the two or three small steamers which had got up to Nasiriyeh during the flood would give them a tow. Among this small Nasiriyeh fleet, cut off from the Tigris till the next year's flood, was a river gunboat. These flat-bottomed monitors were of two classes: the smaller, known as "fly-boats," being of shallow draught and mounting a four-inch gun in addition to machine-guns; the larger class were more powerfully engined and armed with two six-inch guns. The fleet consisted of five large and twenty small boats, all manned by officers and bluejackets of the Royal Navy. The material for the "fly-boats" was shipped from England and the vessels built at Abadan. The larger class, which had been optimistically designed for the Danube, were towed out to the Gulf. It was possible only for the "fly" class to get up to Nasiriyeh in the floods.

With a favourable wind we covered the hundred miles back to Busrah in an hour and a quarter. The next day I left Busrah by air at 2.50 p.m., and, helped by a south wind, was at Sheikh Saad by 5.10 p.m., a somewhat different passage to my first voyage up. This was the first of many a flight up and down the Tigris. Aeroplanes had hitherto been sent to the front packed in barges, thus utilising valuable tonnage. This had been on account of the authorities' fear of forced landings and the probable loss of machines, and even pilots; practice showed that delivery by air was a safe enough and more efficient method.

As soon as I had left Nasiriyeh the G.O.C. wired that he expected to be attacked on the 8th, and that an aeroplane would be of the greatest assistance. They had as yet no petrol or oil at Nasiriyeh, so Lieutenant Somers-Clarke left Aircraft Park at Busrah with one light tender of supplies, a couple of men and a machine-gun. He went by rail as far as Gabashieh, the railhead sixty miles west of Busrah, and thence by desert route south

A "Fly Ship"

Transporting Troops up the Tigris

of the floods to Nasiriyeh, arriving there without opposition, a performance not unattended by risk.

The first week in October the squadron moved forward to Arab Village, less one Flight at Sheikh Saad for bombing work and the detachment *en route* for Nasiriyeh. The supply of oil and stores for the latter detachment continued to be limited on account of the difficulties of the fifty-mile journey across desert from the railhead, but improvement was expected with the advance of the railway and the autumn floods in the Hamar Lake, which made the channel navigable for river steamers.

On the 6th October the R.N.A.S. kite balloon broke away in a strong squall with two officers in the basket, and drifted into the desert. An aeroplane went in search, located it, and remained flying round as guard till cavalry arrived. On the same night one of our machines did not return from reconnaissance. Captain Herring, who was out searching, located it by moonlight; his Very light was answered by the pilot signalling up with an electric lamp that all was "O.K." A guard of six men and an officer went to the rescue by motorcar.

When the white man chooses to penetrate into regions and climates which were made for a different humanity, he will surely pay a toll. Heat and sickness make the blood run thin, and for some of us seven active days in the week were seldom realised. After a short time in my tent at Arab Village with fever and dysentery, I was carried forth to a field ambulance, and later a jolty ride in a cavalry ambulance took me to the river steamer, for the medical men had decreed that I was for "down river."

One does not thrive on rice water, and things were looking rather as if the sages at Bombay had been correct, and my little sojourn with Force "D" was over. We lay in rows on the deck in various stages of adversity and weakness, and counted the flies crawling up the awning as the ship chugged downstream. It was mid-October, and the breeze was cool. Four stalwart Gurkhas carried me ashore at Sheikh Saad, where I was put into a hospital tent, and lay faithfully attended by a Hampshire orderly. Of that hospital tent in the desert I seem to remember nothing but waking up with a coating of sand all over my face.

In spite of breathing and swallowing it the brew of rice water must have been good, for things began to look up, and Horlick's Malted Milk and brandy completed the cure, and I soon crawled forth. I went no further down river, but back to the front. The weather by the end of October became cold at night; a hot day would be followed by an immediate drop of twenty degrees, and one would shiver within a few minutes of sweltering in the sun. At noon the temperature was 95 and at night only 40, a difference of 55 degrees! On the morning of the 26th Captain King-Harman and Lieutenant Hayward were killed while starting out on reconnaissance in a Voisin; it was one of those accidents with no evidence to give any clue as to the cause. These splendid fellows were a great loss to the squadron. They lie in the desert close to the Tigris.

The hills far to the East, known as the Pusht-i-Kuh, were the home of warlike Persian nomads, governed by an independent potentate, the *wali* of Pusht-i-Kuh. His political tendencies were uncertain, he loathed the Russians, but at the same time found much profit in supplying the British Army with sheep. His wife was ill, and he employed a German nurse and an English doctor in his winter camp among the foothills. Down the ages Pusht-i-Kuh had never been conquered by any monarchy: Assyrian, Achaemenian, Sassanian, or Arab.

There is little known about this wild, mountainous region which lies away from all main routes. It was necessary to maintain friendly relations with the *wali*, who was a source of supply and also a possible threat on our right flank. To impress him, six of us flew out one fine morning in close formation to locate his camp, a row of different coloured tents, and executed "stunts" over the top. There was obviously great excitement below; it was the first time these folk had seen a flying machine.

The moral effect of our aeroplanes was gradually growing; it must have been with eyes searching the horizon that any Turk or Arab column moved out into the desert. On the 25th October a machine on reconnaissance observed a column of horsemen and mule carts moving south along the Hai. The pilot came down low and dispersed the convoy in all directions. An agent later reported that nine were killed, several wounded, and that the carts, which were loaded with ammunition for Arab levies on the Hai, turned back to Kut after the attack. One morning a report was received from Sheikh Saad that Arabs had raided and ridden off with some of our camels towards the hills. Two machines went in pursuit, and found the party taking cover in the *nullahs*. They were driven out by Lewis gunfire, and, abandoning the camels, rode hard for the foothills. It was fine sport for our men. A squadron of cavalry arriving on the scene regained the camels.

Enemy aircraft were fairly active, and commenced a half-hearted campaign against our aerodrome at Arab Village; they dropped their bombs from a great height, their shooting was inferior. Sometimes one dropping into the river would provide fish for the camp. The old B.E.'s gave chase, but there was small chance of bringing them to action before they got down to their aerodrome at Shumran. Any raid was answered within a few hours by one of double the magnitude. Six or seven of us would go off in formation and, taking our time, bomb Shumran scientifically.

One bomb would be dropped on each run up wind over their hangars and sights corrected each time. Their anti-aircraft fire was inaccurate, and they never attempted to come up and engage. With all this practice the skill of the pilots increased, and the shooting became remarkably accurate. The enemy became dismayed; on the approach of our aeroplanes he would begin "taxying" his own round the aerodrome to make our shooting difficult. It was an interesting spectacle.

"D. H." took especial delight in this persecution of the Hun; he spent hours hung up in the wind on the top of Shumran, spreading "eggs" on the aerodrome, eventually sending down a 20 lb. bomb from 6,000 feet clean through the fuselage of an Albatross on the ground. This was no chance shot but sheer skill, and the reward of long practice. Irrefutable proof of this brilliant shot was gained later in the advance when, captured among other documents of the enemy air unit, was found a snapshot of the wrecked machine with German officers standing round it. We learnt the names of some of their pilots. Schutz was a fine fighter, and a gentleman. Sometimes he would drop a note on the aerodrome; he asked us to send over the *Sketch* and the *Bystander*, and stated that they were tired of the records captured with a gramophone at Kut, would we send them some new ones, especially "Tipperary"; in return for this they would drop us fresh vegetables from Baghdad. Unlike the Hun, he seemed a sportsman and possessed a sense of humour. To prisoners he was kind and courteous.

At this time there were many aerial combats, but the Hun would never close, and with only B.E.'s it was impossible to press a decision. Propaganda was also dropped by both sides; the following is a specimen:

(Translation.)
Withdrawal of the Turks From El-Arish.
On the 19th December the Turkish troops occupying El-Arish, on the Egyptian Frontier, were driven out of El-Arish by the English, and on the 23rd a decisive battle was fought at Magdhaba, which is thirty-five kilometres S.E. of El-Arish. The Turkish Force was routed and practically destroyed, and 1,350 prisoners, seven guns, a large number of rifles, 100,000 rounds of gun ammunition, horses, camels, and a quantity of telephones and warlike stores were captured.
Further South-West of this defeat British troops moved through the Milta Pass and destroyed the Turkish defences at the Eastern end and burnt their camps at Sudral-Hoitan, about sixty kilometres East of Suez.
Observe how the Germans are powerless to aid their friends. They are asking for peace because they are at the end of their resources; on the other hand, the English strength is now beginning to reach its full development.

We learnt more of the enemy from exchanged prisoners, as two armistices were arranged for the latter purpose. Suspension of arms would take place from 4 a.m. till 7 p.m., a flag of truce was shown over the trenches at Sannayat, and a British staff officer met a Turkish officer in "No Man's Land." The Turkish and British officers would board a river steamer full of Turkish prisoners, which would then proceed past the lines as far as the Magasis Bend, where the sick were exchanged, either party being prevented from looking out by side curtains round the ship. Though rigid formality was observed on these occasions, conversation would be carried on in French, it was a field day for the Intelligence Department.

Some jolly days were spent in the desert practising co-operation with other arms. The squadron possessed several useful remounts, and "Anzac," "Bert," and others would ride out with me, fifteen miles there and fifteen miles back in the clear, crisp weather, to assist from the ground. Returning to the camp in the late afternoon and sitting down to a large meal gave one the same glorious feeling that comes after a day's hunting.

On 7th November there was a cloud in the sky, the first we had seen since our arrival in the country- three and a half months before. It was a fluffy white blob of cumulus about 5,000 ft. up. I got into my machine and climbed into it; it was good to be in the mist again. Later in the day there was a shower of rain.

I made one more visit to Nasiriyeh by air. German aeroplanes had never been seen over the place, but as I was starting off in a car to have a look at the ruins of Ur (of the Chaldees) the drone of two Mercedes engines was unmistakable overhead. I had come in a new Martinsyde, and dashing back to the aerodrome got off and chased up the Euphrates. But the Huns had gone back to Kut by the Hai, where they apparently came from. We had suspected them from Samawa. I lost a good chance, for my machine had the legs of them. Curiously enough, among papers captured later was found a photograph taken from these aeroplanes on this visit. On the back was the date, and on the ground was my machine. I have that photograph.

By the end of the month a stream of reinforcements had arrived up the Tigris, and a large concentration of stores and war material had been accumulated at Sheikh Saad, the Advanced Base. The 13th Division returned to the Front, and with the 14th formed another corps under General Marshall, who had arrived from Salonika. There were now two corps, the 1st and 3rd; by some trick of officialdom there was no second corps. About this time G.H.Q. moved from Busrah and came up river to a standing camp at Arab Village, nicknamed "the White City." The weather was cool, comparing favourably with a fine spring at home; our health was good and spirits splendid, for it looked as though further developments were intended in Mesopotamia.

CHAPTER 3

The Battles That Won Baghdad

'Tis all a Checquered-Board of Nights and Days
Where Destiny with Men for Pieces plays;
Hither and thither moves, and mates, and slays,
And one by one back in the Closet lays.
                                    —Omar.

One morning an orderly came to my office on the barge bidding me to a conference at G.H.Q. I remember the scene so well; we went into a tent, dark after the glare outside, and waited there for General Maude, a strong sense of coming events hanging over us. Here, gathered together in the gloom, were the heads of departments to be told the future plans for an Army tried to its utmost by heat, disease, inaction; fretting against what it felt to be a stain, the fall of Kut, and longing to be at the Turk again. The ill effects of the hot weather had been shaken off and the troops renewed by health and reinforcements, and, spurred by the great deeds of their brothers in France, were spoiling for a fight.

The facts were put clearly before us: the 3rd Corps on the right bank was to move and secure possession of the Hai river, whilst the 1st Corps bombarded the Turkish trenches on the left bank, to give the impression that an attack on Sannayat was intended. Bigger events vaguely hinted at would doubtless follow; perhaps another patch of red was to be added to the map. With the great secret we emerged into the sunlight; the die was cast, and in two days' time the British Army would move. Meanwhile no curiosity must be aroused among the force or inevitably it would reach the Turk. Both sides continued with their stagnant blockade.

On the afternoon of the 12th December the army knew; after eight months' inaction the effect was electrifying.

That evening the 3rd Corps marched and concentrated in the forward area on the right bank. The movement was carried out under cover of night; no tents were put up next morning, and the troops were kept hidden away in *nullahs*. General Headquarters moved out to Sinn, on the right bank, leaving the "White City" standing at Arab Village. I flew Brigadier-General Lewin low along the Hai river to examine the banks for the crossing of his 40th Brigade the next day. The Sannayat position was heavily bombarded to give the impression that an attack was intended, and the sudden gunfire must have come as a surprise to the Turk after the many long uneventful months.

The anti-aircraft system of observation posts, wireless and telephone calls had been perfected, for one Hun over our lines would have exposed our movements; it was an anxious time, and pilots sat in their machines ready to leave at the word "Go!" An Aviatik that came out to ascertain what was up, was chased back over his lines by Paddy Maguire, who closed to a hundred and fifty yards and let him have a drum of ammunition; the Hun went down to his own country in a steep dive. That was their only effort during the day, and our concentration on the right bank remained undetected.

The cavalry division, encamped opposite our aerodrome on the other side of the river, were to move that night. I went over in my motor-launch to see some friends before they left and to make any final aerial arrangements necessary. They were in fine fettle and glorious spirits; the officers packing their kits and donning their equipment as happy as schoolboys off for the holidays. Life was good. They marched after dark.

The enemy's bridge of boats spanned the Tigris at Shumran; if this could be cut he would be without efficient means of reinforcing his troops on the right bank when our move was discovered. That night three of us attacked the bridge with heavy bombs from 600 feet; a pontoon bridge is a narrow mark; we hit a pontoon but did not cut it. There was a bright moon, and to avoid detection we made a detour round the Suwaikieh Marsh, approaching Shumran from the North. I made for what seemed the bend in the river which marks Shumran, but it proved to be a similar bend twenty miles higher up; by the time I got back to the Turkish bridge it was light in the East, and my attack was made under a heavy fire.

The beauty of the flight back was ethereal; the morning clear and cold, the sky cloudless. To the North shone the snows of the Persian hills; ahead the Tigris wound into the approaching day and then toppled over the horizon as if on the lip of some great waterfall; to the right lay the Hai river like a long wriggling snake; and behind was the gloom of the fast-vanishing night. High up in that wonderful dawn it seemed that the aeroplane was stationary, the movement so smooth; one sang for the very joy of living, and the song harmonised with the rhythmic hum of the engine. Far below the *nullahs* and trenches occupied by the enemy were disclosed by the charcoal fires on which they cooked their coffee. The situation was as plain as draughts on a board; it all seemed so simple.

The cavalry division and part of the 3rd Corps had crossed the Hai without opposition by 6 a.m., and were moving northwards up that river. The enemy's advanced troops were surprised and driven back on to a strongly-held entrenched position. Two pontoon bridges which had been brought across the desert from Arab Village were thrown across the Hai at Atab and Basrugi-yeh.

Our cavalry out on the flank reconnoitred almost to the Tigris above Shumran, and Sannayat was again bombarded to confuse the Turk. The squadron spent the day in the air, maintaining contact and communication with our far-flung line, watching for an artillery opportunity, attacking parties of the enemy, and on distant reconnaissance. Mac, on his pony, met machines as they landed at the advanced ground at Sinn, and after close examination of the pilot and observer, galloped back to deliver the reports direct to the army commander. G.H.Q. were thus enabled to keep in touch even to the furthest cavalry patrol, with a situation which otherwise must have been obscure. I spent the typical day of an air commander, immersed in a sea of maps and MSS., glued to a telephone receiver.

These records are no place for technical details, but the lay reader may not know that an aero-engine can only run a certain number of hours without overhaul; in our case it was usually a hundred hours. It was impossible to forecast for how long this full power would be required by the army; economy in the use of machines was therefore essential. The conditions on the Western Front were different. There an aeroplane could be replaced in a night; a wire was sent and a new pilot and machine would arrive next morning. A pilot did six to nine months at the Front, after which, if he survived, he returned to England for a spell of other work.

In Mesopotamia there were a few reserve machines at Amara and Busrah which could be flown up in, say, a couple of days by pilots sent back from the front; outside these the nearest source of supply was Egypt, three weeks away! There was no certainty of any relief owing to high demand elsewhere, and a fresh man from England might take anything up to eight or ten weeks to reach us. The Mediterranean route had been closed, so troops and material came half-way round the world, via the Cape, with perhaps long delays at Durban and Bombay. It frequently happened that reliefs went sick at one of these places, or even after getting so far as Busrah, and never reached us at all.

The overworked, feverish individual, anxiously carrying on with visions of England, Home and Beauty, would, after an extra whiskey-and-soda, resign himself to his fate, and with the sympathy of his fellows go off again on reconnaissance "for the millionth time," still praying that his luck might hold till perhaps someday fresh blood reached the Squadron. It can be understood then how necessary it was to husband our resources, and in these opening days of action there was the greatest difficulty in restraining eager pilots. Work—there was work for three squadrons, but in December, 1916, the Western Front absorbed new units ere they were hardly formed. We had to manage as best we could.

It was common in the great deeds perpetrated in France for the best part of a squadron to be put out of action before nightfall. Here in this far land, where, without aerial observation, shot might as well not be fired; where maps were insufficiently accurate for troops to march by; and where, unless guarded and forewarned by the Air unit, men might walk into unknown and ambushed *nullahs*; it would have been a sorry tale to tell G.H.Q. that there could be no flying on the morrow because of casualties today. The risks had to be taken and we backed our luck; it never failed. A feature of the country that considerably promoted the efficiency of close co-operation was the fact that a good pilot could generally land by the unit itself, give them their accurate position and inform the commander of the situation personally. It was done on many occasions.

On this first day of fighting, enemy aircraft made another attempt to come out, but was met over Kut by D. H., who chased it down on to its own aerodrome in a steep nose-dive; whereupon, taking steady aim, he dropped a bomb which dropped only ten yards from its tail as soon as it had landed.

In the evening a message came through that Lieutenants Chabot and Browning had been forced to land in front of our cavalry with a main strut shot away. For the benefit of the fresh air I flew out with a spare in order to get them back. The sun was setting as I arrived over the rearmost patrols, retiring by troops to their positions for the night; I could see Arab horsemen, showing up well in their flowing garments, hovering about on the flanks; I could also see the damaged aeroplane being dragged back by the cavalry.

The ground was very broken, and it was necessary to land among the rear party, who were retiring steadily in open formation. As I came low one of the horses took fright, threw its *sowar*, and bolted, dragging the rider over the stony ground; he must have been killed. Events moved rapidly. It had been my intention to land, hand them the strut to take back to the machine, and clear off without stopping my engine. But the engine unfortunately stopped as I landed. A *sowar* galloped up and took the strut while I endeavoured to start the engine singlehanded. The last few *sowars*, thinking I was about to start, were retiring past me to the right and left, occasionally turning round to fire back at the *Buddoos* (Arabs), who were blazing off their old *bundooks* and spitting up the sand all round.

It was rapidly growing dark, and the situation was unpleasant; in a moment I should be alone with these howling savages all round. As I was exerting my best strength to start the propeller, a British officer fortunately came galloping back. Major Secker, of the 14th Hussars; he had been an aerial observer in France. I leapt into my seat and he started me off, thereby saving an awkward situation. The damaged aeroplane was never recovered; the cavalry dragged it five miles, but to do so had to hack off its wings; the machine had to be left outside protection on account of a deep *nullah* filled with water; when the engine was regained it had been damaged beyond repair by Arabs.

That night of the 14th/15th December, Captain Herring went out on a moonlight reconnaissance to trace any move the enemy might contemplate under cover of darkness. He discovered that the Turkish pontoon bridge had been dismantled, and was being towed in sections further upstream by a steamer. As a result of the continual bombing the steamer repeatedly slipped her tow, and the pontoons drifted down into the banks; the steamer went ashore herself several times.

The pilot twice returned to Arab Village to replenish his bombs, and the same thing happened again. As a result the steamer accomplished nothing for six hours. Captain Herring dropped twenty-four bombs during the night from a height of from two to four thousand feet, under continuous rifle fire. The day broke to find the enemy without communication between their forces on either bank, and the pontoons were not collected or the river bridged till later in the day. It was an achievement of great magnitude for one individual.

Up till the 18th, the 3rd Corps gradually advanced north-west, keeping pressure on the enemy's Hai position. Our aeroplanes, co-operating with the artillery, succeeded in destroying their pontoon bridges over the Hai, besides engaging many other targets. The work went on with vigour, and the enemy was harassed night and day. From midnight till dawn of the 16th he was kept awake; his camps were bombed and machine-gunned, two bombs making direct hits on barges. Lieutenant Windsor, on the night of the 18th, hit a steamer, the explosion loosened her moorings, and the current swung her round on to a bank. It was rumoured that Khalil Pasha, the G.O.C. of the Turkish army, had been on board *en route* down river from Bghailah. During the day any column that was caught in the desert would almost certainly be spotted and attacked from the sky, its horses stampeded and casualties inflicted. Tents hit by bombs were demolished, and in one camp a bomb exploded in the centre of a crowd of 200 men.

On the 18th the cavalry division operating westward, above Shumran, drove the enemy from his trenches and shelled his shipping. Having marched at night, owing to complete lack of landmarks great difficulty was experienced in finding their way, and care was necessary to prevent blundering on to the river at the wrong place, or into a Turkish position. Our aeroplanes would find them halted, and land to give them their position, which was often a few miles different to their calculation. A hundred feet up and everything was obvious, but once on the ground even the pilot who had just descended might lose his bearings.

The same day the 3rd Corps gained the river bank opposite Kut, thus severing the Turkish position on the right bank and isolating the garrison in the Khadairi bend, who had the river behind them and only a few pontoons for communication with the other side. An Aviatik was out on the 19th, but he was chased by D. H., and after a short running fight dived for his own aerodrome.

On the 20th the cavalry carried out another raid to the Tigris above Shumran, and a column of all arms endeavoured to bridge the river while the Kut and Sannayat areas were heavily bombarded. This column, after a long night march with the bridging train, arrived to find the far bank strongly entrenched; a gallant attempt was made to launch the pontoons in the face of a heavy fire till they were ordered to withdraw.

These raids were a constant threat to the enemy's communications as far as thirty miles behind his Sannayat position and must have been a continual source of anxiety to the higher command. D. H. and I spent the afternoon bombing camps and shipping at Bghailah, a small town forty-five miles by river above Kut. A 336 lb. bomb rather spoilt the appearance of the river-front, and the persecution of a tug under weigh caused her crew to run her ashore and abandon her.

Over Shumran, Lieutenant Merton sighted an Albatross at about 800 yards range. The hostile machine dived for his aerodrome, but Merton gained, and closing to a range of fifty yards opened fire; the hostile observer was hit and collapsed over his gun, and the machine went down in a vertical dive. Merton held on, firing close behind; the enemy hit the ground heavily, bounced up again, then landed, apparently without being totally wrecked. By this time Merton, who was at a height of only 2,000 feet, came under heavy rifle and machine-gun fire from the ground; his engine was badly hit, and he only just managed to land inside our advanced lines on the Hai. An agent reported the enemy observer killed, the pilot wounded, and the machine crashed. Later on, at Baghdad, we found the fuselage of this aeroplane in the workshops; the observer's cockpit was drenched with blood.

Consolidation of our position on the Hai went on; the cavalry division were ever on the move harassing the Turkish communications and making punitive raids on Arab encampments; marching by night and skirmishing by day sorely tried the horses. It was a hard life for the cavalry. But the enemy would not move; General Maude must have hoped that his threat to their communications would cause Khalil Pasha to make some move from Sannayat and give him an opening; Khalil Pasha sat doggedly firm.

The air offensive went on; a ton of bombs was dropped on Bghailah on the 21st, and three machines again visited the place that night; the work of registration from all the new artillery positions allowed no respite. On Christmas Eve the cavalry attacked and burnt the Arab stronghold Gussabs Fort, and D. H. reconnoitred the river as far as Baghdad; it was the first time since the battle of Ctesiphon that a British aeroplane had been over the city; we heard later what consternation it caused. He came back with wonderful tales of gardens and vegetation, railway station, tram-lines, and buildings it sounded all very civilised to us in the desert.

Christmas Day, 1916, in Mesopotamia was I expect much more cheerful than in England; work was reduced to a minimum, and a great feast had been prepared, after which, heavily laden with good food and drink, the squadron held athletic sports. It was a day full of fun, officers from every unit wandering round each other's camps and exchanging greetings. The Force was a happy family; men under these conditions get to know and understand each other in a different fashion to normal times; on active service there can be little convention or artificiality; the soul is stripped, and the man stands out in a genuine form for better or for worse.

Life-long friendships are founded in a short space of time; in the ordinary humdrum days of peace and security we are apt to pass by some of the greater bounties of Life. Bobby had invented a special dope for the occasion, and the mess was packed with merry individuals. One could hardly see across the tent in the thick fog of tobacco smoke; song and chorus rang out. The cheer of the day was kept up far into the night.

The weather broke at last; operations had been purposely hurried on before the commencement of the rains, for the terrible experiences of the previous year, when the country was flooded most of the winter, and the wounded were even drowned before it was possible to pick them up, were still fresh to our minds. Rain converted the country into a quagmire, and it was well known that any operations would be stopped thereby. The weather was a more difficult proposition to General Maude than the Turk, and it must have been with sad misgivings that the G.O.C. saw the clouds bank up and heard the deluge splash down on his tent.

For many weeks we had been collecting from down-river all the date-palm matting, known as *chittai*, that could be squeezed on to the already overladen barges, with the idea of spreading it over the aerodrome to give the wheels of the machines a grip when the wet weather came; unfortunately our labours were useless, for the experiment proved unsuccessful. High southerly winds and rain during the last weeks in December and the first week of the New Year flooded the country, but flying took place whenever possible in order to continue the work of mapping the country behind the lines, for registration of targets and reconnaissance. Two hangars were blown down, but the machines saved. The river rose eight feet in a fortnight, and all hands were turned on to the construction of *bunds* to keep it from inundating the entire country, which would have left the British force in a sorry plight.

There are two periods of flood in the Tigris and Euphrates; the first starts about the second week in November, and is caused by the autumn rains in the hills, the volume varying each year according to the wetness of the season; the second comes down in April as a result of the snows melting in the Caucasus, and is the greatest, not subsiding until June. Then the rivers course past in a yellow spate, against which it is difficult for any craft to make headway; the waters drop until they are about their lowest in August, September, and October. It is hard for the persecuted white man, in the furnace of a Mesopotamian June, to imagine the thick flood racing past as the thaw off glaciers a thousand miles away.

The period of bad weather was not altogether unwelcome to the R.F.C., for it gave us a breathing space in which to over-

KHADAIRI BEND, DAHRA BEND, HAI SALIENT AND SHUMRAN

haul aeroplanes and engines, relieve personnel due for England by drafts arrived at Busrah, and allow pilots and observers a rest from the intensive flying that had been going on.

The enemy had taken up a strong position in the Khadairi bend on the right bank of the Tigris, where he meant to stay; it was important that we should move him, as he could open the *bund* and in a high flood cut our communications to the Hai, which were being linked by an extension of the light railway from Sinn. The 3rd Division had a slow and difficult task before them,[1] as, like most fighting in Mesopotamia, it lay across open country; there was no cover except a fringe of scrub along the left flank. The rain had stopped by the 6th January, and the British troops worked hard sapping out to the Turkish position. On the 9th, after a sharp hand-to-hand fight, Gurkhas and Mahrattas reached the river, while on the right the Manchesters and 59th Rifles succeeded, against fog and counter-attack, in clearing the trenches and *nullahs*, incurring heavy loss on the enemy.

From here an attempt made during the next two days to drive the Turks out of their position failed owing to our attacking parties being enfiladed from both sides; but the Highland Light Infantry had forced the enemy back, steel to steel and inch by inch, only a remnant living to tell the tale of their glory in the depot at Hamilton. A week was spent constructing covered approaches and assembly trenches from which to launch the final assault. The fighting for the enemy's advanced posts was severe; redoubts were lost and won several times over; by the 18th the last one had fallen. We got ready for the supreme effort on the morrow, which was to clear the enemy out of the Khadairi bend; a message dropped from the air asked him to surrender, but during the night he retired across the river, leaving us masters of the situation.

On account of the weather the co-operation of the R.F.C. in this fighting was of little help; gaps in the mist afforded only occasional chances for the artillery spotters. Three machines were held up at the advanced ground at Sinn one stormy night; the

---

1. See sketch map.

next morning, though clear at Sinn, there was a thick fog at Arab Village, and it was only just in time that a message got through stopping them from attempting the passage. A possible catastrophe narrowly averted.

The 1st Corps now cleared the enemy from the east bank of the Hai, and to the west the 3rd Corps advanced another mile. Gradually we were creeping forward towards his communications, but the price was heavy.

A reorganisation of the R.F.C. took place. MacEwen's appointment as Assistant-Director of Aeronautics was abolished, and he unfortunately left us. D. H. took command of the squadron, and I set up my headquarters at Sinn.

The Hai salient was the next series of fortifications barring our progress against the enemy's communications.[2] This salient was defended by the most effective gun emplacements and a strong trench system. From the 25th the fighting to clear the Turk from the right bank was terrific; the gallantry on both sides was great and the casualties telling. By the 26th we had secured a firm foothold in his first-line trenches. A Flight was detached to Sinn to co-operate with the 3rd Corps in this offensive. They had become artists in artillery co-operation, and flew till their eyes hung heavy in their heads. The enemy air force became more active and much bolder; new blood seemed to have arrived among them. Day after day Merton and his men would go up with a long and difficult artillery programme and the certainty of interruption; yet neither Weather nor Boche interfered with the achievement of this Flight, which accomplished the work of a squadron.

On the 27th January, Lieutenant Baldwin and "Anzac," in a B.E., were attacked by a Fokker and Albatross; their petrol tank was blown open and engine hit, but "Anzac" drove off both Huns with his rear gun, damaging one so that it dived for home. Our machine managed to land the right side of the line. On the 20th January, a raid of three machines had gone to Baghdad and bombed the citadel, completely wrecking a workshop and some houses.

2. See sketch map.

The cavalry division marched back to Arab Village in order to operate against the enemy's rear round the north of the Suwaikieh Marsh, *via* Bedrah and Jessan, a surprise movement to synchronise with the attack of the 3rd Corps on the Hai. The scheme entailed long desert marching, the man-handling of guns and wagons over rough country, and difficulties of supply and communication. It was ambitious, but had it succeeded the results might have been far-reaching, for the enemy's position at Sannayat must have been imperilled. General Maude explained the operations to me personally; the Turk having, so far, not moved an inch from Sannayat in spite of our threats in his rear, we must try something fresh, perhaps this would shift him.

Luck was against us. The cavalry had got well out on their night march when a heavy thunderstorm burst; the ground became a marsh and the dry *nullahs* rushing torrents; guns and limbers sank in to their axles; horses floundered, and in the inky darkness progress in either direction was impossible. The attempt was abandoned; with the coming of the dawn they extricated themselves, and, drenched to the skin and worn out, regained Arab Village.

The struggle on the Hai continued. On February 1st the two armies swayed backwards and forwards in fierce conflict. Just before the zero hour "Bobby" and Lieutenant Beevor-Potts were directing the final storm of artillery fire before it lifted for our men to go over, when a Fokker came down like a thunderbolt on their tail. Bobby turned sharp, and the German passed in front of him, so seizing the opportunity he made his machine sit up on its tail and got his forward gun to bear. The Hun went down in one last long dive, turning over and over like a leaf. A cloud of dust, smoke, and flame marked his pyre just behind the Turkish front line.

Our army, crouching down below with rifle and bayonet ready for the assault, had been watching the duel. Bobby had chosen his moment well. They went over with a yell of triumph, the Cheshires on the east bank cleared the enemy from their trenches and succeeded in stopping there. On the west bank the

SUNSET ON THE TIGRIS

OUR MULE TRANSPORT

AN AERODROME IN THE RAINS

battle was grim. The 36th and 45th Sikhs charged across the open, raked by machine-gun fire from their left flank, and captured the Turkish trench. They met the counter-attack in the open with a glorious charge; the conflict was hand-to-hand. Forced back by sheer weight of numbers, stabbing and clubbing the enemy, these bearded warriors retired, but only a small remnant of the two splendid battalions regained their own trenches.

The 3rd Corps extended their line north-west, and a renewal of the attack on the 3rd gained us the first two lines of enemy trenches. On this day Lieutenants Baldwin and Hannay forced an Aviatik to land near Bghailah; it was reported later that the pilot had been wounded. The last of the enemy on the east of the Hai withdrew to the west, and during the night of the 4th fell back to the Liquorice Factory and a line across the Dahra Bend in the Tigris.[3] They had lost heavily in dead and prisoners, besides the arms, ammunition and stores that we had captured. Their hold on the right bank of the Tigris was being wrested from them, and further possibilities were opening out; our troops were in fine fettle. A parade of the remnant of the 36th and 45th Sikhs was held, and General Maude made a speech in English, which was then translated and delivered in Hindustani.

Sinn was conveniently situated midway between the two corps in the Sannayat and Hai areas. Here, in rows of little forty-pound tents, lived the Headquarter Staff. A forty-pound tent is an economical form of housing, and can be packed up and carried away at a moment's notice; yet it is a warm and comfortable domain when the interior has been dug down four feet to give head room and keep out draught. There is just sufficient space for a camp bed, and the double layer of canvas keeps out sun and rain. It was characteristic of General Maude that he should live under the same conditions as the rest of the army; he never considered his personal comfort, and refused to allow himself extra luxury by reason of high office. His thoughts were ever with the rank and file and the arrangements for their welfare. There might be a limited supply of oil stoves for the winter, but

---

3. See sketch map

General Maude and his staff would shiver among their maps and papers till a sufficient supply had first been provided for those he considered more in need. There was no extra provision for G.H.Q. in Mesopotamia.

It was a happy camp at Sinn; the weather was bracing; the work hard and the life active and healthy for all except those whose misfortune tied them completely to an office. On a quiet evening there were black partridge in the scrub, or sniping the Turk across the river from behind sandbags in Magasis Fort; or, after a long day's work, an evening ride into the desert to restore the brain-weary staff officer. The wire fencing and block-house system south of the railway was carried on to the Hai to keep the Arab raiders out of the occupied area; but, in spite of every device, they would get through and back between the block-houses with even camels and tents.

The Flight at Sinn were a few minutes' gallop from my own headquarters, so that within twenty minutes I could be at any point by air, and a wireless station rigged at the office tent enabled me to listen to the machines working on the line. Hertzian waves were as food and drink to "Huxley," my wireless officer, a most progressive individual.

The Turkish Force on the right bank of the Tigris were now confined entirely to the Liquorice Factory and Dahra Bend. The initiative remained in the hands of General Maude, and he never gave them a chance to wrest it away.

Carrying straight forward after the victory on the Hai, the Liquorice Factory was fiercely bombarded, and on the 9th February the whole line was attacked. The Worcesters and King's Own both captured the enemy's line at different points, out of which the Turks failed to dislodge them. The next day the Factory fell, and we gradually closed in on the enemy, who had retired to a second line across the bend. Strong south-easterly winds and heavy rain retarded progress and made aerial reconnaissance difficult, but on the 10th, in spite of these conditions, an aeroplane directing a sixty-pounder gun damaged the enemy bridge over the Tigris at a range of 9,800 yards, and sunk a barge more than five miles away.

The aerodrome at Sinn and Arab Village became a marsh, but on only one day was flying actually impossible. On this day the Corps H.Q. rang up Merton's Flight and enquired if he was sending anything up; Captain Merton replied that his present difficulty in the raging gale was keeping his machines on the ground. The state of the ground further hindered the supply of rations and ammunition along our ever-lengthening line of communication.

For three days all our guns were concentrated against the enemy's left, and on the 15th a feint attack brought down his barrage on our right, thus disclosing the massing of his artillery, as we had desired, on that point of the line. Then the 3rd Corps, launching their main attack against the centre, carried all before it. The Turks tried to reinforce the centre from their left, where the main body was collected, but our barrage made this impossible. For three days the plan had been elaborated; its success was complete.

The enemy attempted to escape across the river, but few reached the other side. The R.F.C. were waiting in the sky, and the artillery had the range of every ferry point. Bomb and shell tore the pontoons, and the flood did the rest. By the 16th February the Dahra Bend was cleared and 2,000 prisoners had been captured. It was a night of great rejoicing. D. H. celebrated the occasion by obtaining a direct hit on a steamer at Bghailah.

What would be our next move and how far were we to be allowed to go? Force "D" awaited the word of its chief like hounds straining at the leash. Torrential rain on the 16th and 17th did its best to damp their ardour; camps, trenches, bivouacs, and aerodromes were flooded, canvas hangars could not keep it out and aeroplanes became saturated.

The British Force, after two months' hard fighting, had swept the Turk entirely off the right bank of the Tigris. To close with him again we must either cross the river or come to grips frontally against his lines at Sannayat. He had worked for a year making this position into a maze of successive lines of trenches on

LOOKING UP THE TIGRIS FROM ARAB VILLAGE

THE LINES AT SANNAYAT BETWEEN MARSH AND RIVER
FROM THE BRITISH SIDE

a narrow front, firmly secured by river and marsh on the flanks. The way seemed effectively barred on the left bank; but for forty miles from Sannayat to Shumran our force was a constant threat on his flank, and the 3rd Corps, opposite Shumran, were very near his communications. Yet Khalil showed no sign of stirring. Perhaps he relied on the impregnability of Sannayat or the sodden condition of the country and further rain to immobilise the rest of the British Army? The experience of the previous year would almost justify his reasoning. Perhaps he considered a surprise crossing in strength an impossible contingency. The river was sweeping down in full spate, it would be a long and hazardous operation to bridge it; meanwhile sufficient force could be concentrated at the threatened point. So Khalil waited.

General Maude intended to cross the river as far west as possible; it was therefore important to keep the enemy's attention about Sannayat, and orders were issued to the 1st Corps to attack on the 17th February. It was a year since Sannayat had been attacked; the same troops who had thrown themselves at the enemy in vain endeavour to break through to Kut, had held the same ground for eleven months, sweated through the hot weather, and were now in the trenches waiting for the signal to attack. To ensure surprise there was no artillery preparation; a short tornado on their wire, and the guns would lift for the assault.

I remember waiting in suspense outside my office tent for the opening crash. The two aeroplanes for locating active enemy guns were humming high above, having made a detour preparatory to turning down wind over Sannayat on time, no earlier. Suspicion must not be aroused. It was a peaceful afternoon, the desert green with recent rain and heavy banks of cloud threatening further downpour. One thought of the men fixing their bayonets in the trenches and their hearts hammering off the last few minutes. Suddenly great spurts of desert began flying in the air, and the booming of cannon rolled across the intervening plain to where I was watching; Hell had descended on Sannayat.

I was glued to my telephone when General Maude, standing close outside, came in to talk to the 1st Corps H.Q. The Gurkhas and Punjabis had captured the first two lines on a narrow frontage with little loss, but were being heavily counter-attacked. The men from India and Nepal were unable to withstand the onslaught, and most of their British officers had been killed. The general urged that a British battalion should be sent in at once. The Black Watch, ordered to support, were baulked in getting out of their trenches by the rush of native troops tumbling back in. The enemy regained his lost line, except for a small party of Gurkhas on the river bank, who stuck there till dusk. At least these operations had turned the enemy's attention to Sannayat.

The next day D. H., while at his customary occupation of bombing the enemy aerodrome, was interfered with by a Fokker which had ascended to try conclusions with him. The Martinsyde scout out-manoeuvred the German, who, spattered by bullets, went down vertically like a stone, one wing carried away and the rest buried itself in the ground 7,000 feet below. The German aviators watched the duel from their aerodrome, but no other candidate accepted the challenge.

Daily artillery barrages were put down on Sannayat in order to keep confusing Khalil and induce him to accept these, unaccompanied by infantry attacks, as part of our usual routine. When all seemed quiet and peaceful, these intense bombardments would suddenly rend the air at any time of the day. The long six-inch guns of the naval flotilla in the river would chime in as double bass to the general racket, and Sannayat would be obliterated in a fog of flying sand, debris and smoke. The behaviour of the Turkish gunners on these occasions was remarkable. From the air we could see them continue fighting their guns in the most gallant fashion, keeping up a rapid fire in spite of their pits being blown up all round them.

All the time, secretly, quietly, methodically, General Maude prepared for the passage of the Tigris about Shumran, twenty miles away. The river was in highest flood, and the country waterlogged, but drying. All movement and work was carried out under cover of night. Pontoon rowers were selected and trained, men of Norfolk and Hampshire; Gurkhas and Norfolks were to be landed; the tiny Gurkhas, too small to row the pontoons, had to be rowed; their heads barely appeared above the gunwale.

Again, on the 22nd, Sannayat was assaulted after a terrific bombardment. The Seaforths and 92nd Punjabis, with few casualties, found themselves in possession of a wrecked front line. The aero-artillery co-operation blew the Turkish counter-attacks to bits as fast as they formed. The Leicesters, 51st and 53rd Sikhs supported and extended to the right. By nightfall our men had dug themselves in opposite the enemy's fourth line and consolidated the position. A hundred and ten miles away at Baghdad they heard it on the wire, and the German population started packing their baggage. That night the British Army, flushed with their taste of success, learnt of the plans for the morrow; after a year a decision was to be forced.

While the battle had been raging at Sannayat the 3rd Corps were apparently engaged in bridging operations opposite Kut under cover of a heavy bombardment of the town. After dark a party of Punjabis and Sappers pulled across the river at Magasis, raided the Turkish trenches, and returned with a trench mortar as a souvenir. A picquet had been driven in and given the alarm; one can imagine the chaos caused throughout the enemy camps by this sudden appearance of British troops on their side of the river in the middle of the night. This daring bluff by a handful of men across a rushing torrent half a mile wide in inky darkness served its purpose well, and they returned with trifling casualties. Fifteen miles higher up, opposite Shumran, Sappers, Norfolks, Gurkhas, and Gunners looked for the dawn.

Owing to the high flood and consequent difficulties of bridging, it had been decided that the operation by night was impracticable. The "forlorn hope" were to lead over as the darkness turned to grey.

Our barges were loaded; the steamers lay alongside; aeroplanes stood out in readiness to leave the ground; the army awaited the word to trek. We slept lightly that night.

An aerial barrage had been up all day to frustrate any curiosity displayed by the Hun; one had evaded us and learnt all about the activity opposite Kut; special food that had been designed for their consumption; it was well. Orders had been given me by General Maude that no German must leave the ground on the 23rd; co-operation was also essential with all arms, and there was only our one little squadron for the task, but officers and men were told, and were pleased there was no other, for the responsibility remained in their keeping.

Just before the day of the 23rd February the first aeroplanes left the ground; at the same time pontoons, loaded with Norfolks and Gurkhas, pushed out into the flood at three separate points in the Shumran Bend. The first batch of Norfolks using the upstream ferry were practically across in the half-light before the enemy on the other side realised that anything unusual was happening. The two lower ferries, Gurkhas rowed by Hampshires, were met by a hail of bullets and suffered heavily. Some of them, however, succeeded in forcing their way ashore, where they met the Turks hand to hand. An incessant barrage from the British artillery and machine-guns across the river made the enemy keep their heads under cover, and enabled our storming parties to land and assault a loop-holed bund. The casualties became so severe at these two lower ferries, and left so few of the Hampshire rowers alive, that they were both abandoned and the passage confined to the top ferry, which the bend in the river better protected from enfilade. By 7.30 about 700 Norfolks and Gurkhas had established themselves on the far bank; every inch had been fiercely contested at the point of the bayonet; the footing gained enabled the sappers to launch the first pontoon of the bridge. Under peaceful conditions this would have been no small undertaking; there were four hundred yards of a deep five-knot flood to span; in the face of the enemy the task was colossal. The sappers worked like men possessed. The site had been well chosen, the Turkish gunners had no means of locating it, and a Martinsyde scout kept flying round and round their aerodrome to force to the ground any Hun who attempted to leave. This watch on the aerodrome was maintained all day, machines relieving each other on the scene of action. There were only sufficient aeroplanes for one to work at a time, yet our sovereignty of the air was complete till 5 p.m., when one German escaped; but it was too late, the bridge and half a division were across. These pilots, knowing well of the gallant souls dying at the crossing, maintained their lonely beat ceaselessly, unerringly, over the enemy aerodrome. Whenever any activity was displayed away would go a bomb with a whistling sigh and a crash; a dive and a stammering machine-gun finished the work, and the sentry above resumed his beat alone and applauded only by the patter of shrapnel and high explosive. About 11 a.m. an ammunition dump shot up in a cloud of black smoke somewhere opposite Magasis; it was evident that the day was going in our favour, and that the Turk meant to evacuate Sannayat. Here patrols of the 7th Division entered the enemy's third line, but were prevented from advancing further by a strong counter-attack. The enemy evacuated during the night, and the 1st Corps pushed forward, occupying the battered trenches, which were choked with corpses, the ground a shambles of dead and crying wounded. The night was spent in bridging the trenches and clearing a way for the guns and wagons to advance on the morrow.

The bridge at Shumran was completed at 4.30 p.m., and three infantry brigades were across before dark. All night the 3rd Corps poured over a stream of guns, wagons, horses, men, and mules without end. The cavalry division bivouacked close by and looked to their sabres.

The excitement was intense, and all night long G.H.Q. camp buzzed with the subdued sound of work at high pressure. The task of the Supply and Transport service appeared almost insuperable. General Maude, imperturbable as ever, crouching over his maps by the light of a little electric lamp, in the pit of his 40 lb. tent, discussed the plans for next day, and gave me *carte blanche*. An army on the run over flat desert and the complete mastery of the air, one's wildest dream had come true. The weary pilots got

GERMAN AIRMEN ON THE TIGRIS
THIS PHOTOGRAPH WAS CAPTURED DURING
THE ADVANCE TO BAGHDAD

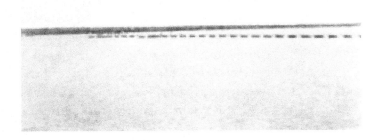

MAUDE'S MASTERSTROKE - THE BRIDGE AT SHURMAN

in to snatch a few hours' sleep, while the mechanics spent the night loading machines with bombs and overhauling engines.

The crossing had been a masterpiece, a clever conception brilliantly carried out. The Turk never knew where the main blow was to fall till too late. By sheer generalship the enemy was outwitted. First the hammer blow at Sannayat induced him to march his reserves in that direction from the Kut area; after marching all night the peril at Shumran became apparent. Khalil ordered them to counter-march, but too late. Maude's tactics kept these reserves marching and counter-marching out of the battle on either front. They were only able to drag themselves clear with the general retreat.

The next day, the 24th February, our troops on the Shumran Peninsula resumed the attack; the enemy fought stubbornly. By nightfall, after severe casualties, we had gained a thousand yards, and the cavalry and practically the whole 3rd Corps were on the other side. The main Turkish Army was in full retreat covered by this tenacious rearguard, who frustrated an attempt by the cavalry to break through and enabled the Sannayat troops to cross our front and get away. In the evening I could see the Horse Artillery of the cavalry division in action against the enemy rearguard, which had withdrawn north-west, and sent down a message to the Divisional H.Q., giving the dispositions.

If the cavalry had only worked further to the north the rearguard would have been outflanked. It was a wonderful sight from the air, the retreat orderly and well controlled, and low-flying aeroplanes came under heavy fire. Flying home over Kut just before dark I met the Gunboat Flotilla coming up full speed from Sannayat, their decks cleared for action, and white ensigns spread out by the breeze made a proud and inspiring picture against the last glow of the Arabian sunset, the battle-line of England surging forward.

Sixteen hundred prisoners, four field guns, and a large number of rifles, ammunition, and stores had been captured. The Turkish rearguard withdrew out of the Shumran Peninsula during the night of the 24th, having effectively covered the westward passage of their army. On the morning of the 25th early reconnaissances located the main body at Bghailah, their rear party with about twenty guns occupying a long *nullah* extending north from the river near Imam Mahdi; to us in the air it seemed inconceivable that the cavalry did not make round the enemy's northern flank; but there they were, immobile down below, held up and being shelled by the Turks. The vanguard of the 13th Division in their stiff fight to eject the enemy from this position nearer the river were helped by the long guns of the navy.

The exhausted cavalry, who had hardly been out of their saddles for forty-eight hours, rode back to water and bivouac; the Turk had given them the slip. General Maude's instructions necessitated reporting every hour by wireless; a field wireless station takes some time to erect and dismantle; perhaps this cramped their commander's movement, but some would have risked incurring displeasure for this chance of a thousand years. After the crossing of the river the ghost of every cavalry leader down the ages must have looked longingly beyond Shumran. For had they ridden hard to the flank they could have gained the river behind the Turks; it seemed even worth the risk of losing their horses, for what has ever been achieved without risk? And the complete obliteration of the Turkish Army was worth more than the cavalry horses. At the end of the day, instead of being behind the Turkish Army the cavalry division were five miles behind their own infantry.

Ninety-four bombs were dropped that day on fleeing Turks and enemy shipping; sixty-five pounders exploding among retreating masses make a grim trail for a pursuing army. D. H. and I found a tug towing sections of the enemy's pontoon bridge. It was a fine target, and the captain of the tug considered it advisable to part with his pontoons, which went drifting downstream while the vessel ran for shore and the crew for cover.

The Turkish retreat was rapid; they threw their guns and heavy encumbrances into the river and ran for all they were worth. On the 26th they outstripped our infantry, who made a forced march across eighteen miles of waterless plain; but Captain Nunn, R.N., with his river flotilla, were racing after them. His orders also had been to report to G.H.Q. hourly by wireless, but Nunn and his men, Commanders Sherbrooke, Buxton, and Cartwright in the *Tarantula, Mantis,* and *Moth,* did the Nelson touch, and crashed on upstream through a hail of Turkish bullets from the banks. At the sharp Nahr Kellak bend they were raked on either side by Turkish batteries and machine-guns, and returned the fire with six-inch guns and Maxims at point-blank range. The quarter-master and Arab pilot of the *Mantis* were both shot dead, and Buxton rushed into the conning-tower just in time to save his ship from taking the bank at fifteen knots. The river here ran alongside the road where the Turkish force was retreating; the guns of the flotilla turned the retreat into a rout, it became *sauve qui peut.*

The flotilla held on, and gradually drawing into range with the flying Turkish river boats brought their bow six-inch guns into action. The rear ship was sunk, and the *Busrah,* with seven hundred wounded and other Turks and Germans on board, was run ashore by a captured and badly-wounded British officer, Lieutenant Cowie, of the Black Watch. Another, the *Pioneer,* burning fiercely but still fighting her guns, ran aground. On went Nunn after the *Firefly* a British gunboat captured in the retreat from Ctesiphon. The navy were intent on getting her back; after a long fight her captain ran her ashore, and she was recaptured.

It was a great day for the Senior Service; they suffered heavy casualties and were riddled by shell and machine-gun fire, but by wonderful fortune none were sunk. Three ships and a thousand prisoners had been captured; one enemy ship sunk; the army routed; and, above all, the lost *Firefly,* or, as the Turks had rechristened her, *Sulman Pak,* recaptured. All that morning General Maude walked up and down wondering what the gunboats were doing, and "why the devil they didn't report as instructed?" That night the navy reported.

The G.O.C. and his staff embarked on board the paddle-boat 53; she had been partitioned off by canvas into the various offices necessary to an advancing and mobile G.H.Q., and arrived at Shumran in the afternoon of the 26th. The squadron occupied the enemy aerodrome. At Kut the Union Jack was flying, having been run up by the bluejackets of the *Mantis* the day before; the town was badly knocked about by shell fire, the result of our recent bombardment and that of the enemy when Townshend was besieged; within it there was no living soul save innumerable cats prowling about among the dead bodies; the stench was nauseating and the silence uncanny.

It was interesting to walk about the enemy aerodrome, which we had known so well from the air, and examine his dug-outs and the holes made by our bombs. The place was littered with fragments, and it was easy to trace the results of one's own shooting on the different occasions. The next morning I witnessed for myself what the gunboats had achieved.

Flying towards Azizieh the, spectacle was amazing and horrible; dead bodies and mules, abandoned guns, wagons and stores littered the road, many of the wagons had hoisted the white flag, men and animals exhausted and starving lay prone on the ground. Few of these, if any, survived the attentions of the Arab tribesmen, hanging round like wolves on their trail. Further on I came up with the rear party on the march.

Flying along about ten feet from the road I mowed down seven with one burst of machine-gun fire; it was sickening; they hardly had the strength to run into the *nullahs* and fire back; those hit just crumpled up under their packs and lay still; others waved in token of surrender and supplication for rescue. All along the road they staggered in twos and threes. Could this have been the fine army to which a British force of seven thousand had surrendered, and which had held us in check for a year? No scene can be so terrible as a routed army in a desert country. I turned home sickened.

The gunboats had hauled in close to the stranded *Busrah*, which was seething with prisoners and flying a large white sheet from the mast. Coming down low I could make out my sailor friends, and dropped them a greeting. It was all perhaps as strange a spectacle as one will ever see in the course of a morning.

In the evening the *Moth, en route* to the base for repairs, ran downstream and anchored for the night at Shumran. I dined on board with Cartwright and heard his story over a bottle of champagne. He had buried two of his crew, but the rest were in magnificent form; he himself and his officers were all wounded, and on the settee lay Cowie of the Black Watch, shot in five places, including the stomach; nevertheless he insisted on toasting the *Moth*: the cupful of champagne almost caused his decease.

He however survived to tell the tale of being blown up by a bomb at Sannayat during a raid the day before the attack, and subsequent nightmare periods of consciousness with the routed Turks; the chase in the *Busrah*, and the British shells through his cabin, the panic aboard, and his assistance in running her ashore though he could barely crawl. We celebrated the glory of the British Navy far into the night, and I can see now the little smoke-filled ward-room, the bandaged naval officers in front of the stove listening to the gramophone; the bullet-holes through the plating and the Highland officer lying on the couch looking mighty pleased with everything. It was life with a big L.

The *Busrah* came down river, the white flag at the fore. One could almost scent her coming. She was packed with wounded Turks, and almost to a man their wounds had turned to gangrene.

On the 1st of March the cavalry reached Azizieh, where the pursuit was broken off. The 3rd Corps and the gunboats concentrated here while the 1st Corps cleared the battlefields and protected the line of march from the Arab hordes who appeared like vultures out of the "blue." The captures since the crossing included: 4,000 prisoners, thirty-nine guns, thirty-two trench mortars, eleven machine-guns, H.M.S. *Firefly*, the river boats *Sumana, Pioneer* and *Busrah*, many barges, and an immense quantity of rifles, ammunition, and stores. Much more material of war lay scattered over the eighty miles of desert, or had been thrown into the river. The enemy streamed on towards Baghdad.

General Maude and his H.Q. on board the P.S. 53 were at Azizieh soon after the cavalry; he towed one of the Flying Corps barges along with him, and the others were pushed up by tugs. The tortuous course of the Tigris and the slow progress against the strong current made it impossible for the squadron transport to keep up with the machines; two fast motorboats and three light lorries, however, usually managed to fetch up at the forward landing ground at night to supply the squadron with fuel. The general had his nose to the trail and pressed forward relentlessly.

The supply services were tried to the breaking point but never broke; it was a marvellous feat of genius in organisation. The base was three hundred and fifty miles away by river, and the return to Sheikh Saad of the stores and ammunition accumulated in the Hai area employed men urgently required at the front. River craft were limited and could only move a certain distance before returning for or awaiting the arrival of fuel. Yet by the 3rd of March one cavalry and three infantry divisions were into Azizieh. If you have seen the fodder necessary for the horses of a cavalry division in one day alone, and realise that every wisp of hay had to be brought from India, it will afford a guide to the colossal achievements of the quartermaster-general and inspector-general of communications.

It seemed doubtful whether the enemy had any aerial force left until Lieutenant Lloyd, on reconnaissance over Baghdad, forced a Fokker down on the aerodrome. On the way up river the old R.F.C. store barge that had been captured at Kut was recaptured. It was laden with German flying stores, engines, and bombs. Fourteen of our machines landed at Azizieh; all hangars and heavy material had been left behind; pilots slept under their planes and carried their food in their pockets. There was an R.F.C. office on board the G.H.Q. ship, where "Chocolo" presided, producing food and drink surreptitiously from the messes of generals for our famished men, who, after long hours in the air, might wait in vain for the uncertain arrival of tins of bully-beef. "Chocolo" became a demi-god, for they were hungry days, and the most friendly units would not trust one another where the acquisition of food was concerned.

The Turkish telegraph wire from Kut to Baghdad had been torn down in their retreat, and lay in festoons on the ground. But the posts were still standing. When no authority was looking the hungry Tommy would cut one down to chop into firewood for his evening meal, the only possible fuel to be found. It became a serious offence, for they were supporting a fresh line behind us. Yet hunger was the matter of the moment, and the marching soldier cared little for the communications in rear when his eyes were on Baghdad. They had to be strictly guarded, else they disappeared uncannily.

The concentration of supplies went on for three days at Azizieh. Even then General Maude had no word from England as to whether he was to advance still further. The pent-up feelings and enthusiasm of the force were boiling over. The men were hard, lean, and fit with the long marching and fighting, and Baghdad shone like an El Dorado in the north with only a routed army between. The name Baghdad was in every mouth, it was the sole topic of conversation, and the army was ready to endure, starve, and die; anything but be told to retire. The brains in Whitehall meanwhile balanced our fate against the memory of Townshend's advance to the walls of the city and his subsequent finale at Kut.

The eagerly awaited orders were issued on the night of the 4th: the British army was to push on.

The 1st Corps had come up, and on the morning of the 5th March, with a swinging step, the expedition went forward. I reconnoitred early as far as the Diala in a gale of wind, which, wiping the dust in dense masses off the ground, obscured observation of the intricate maze of *nullahs*. The cavalry were passing Zeur when I landed in the desert on their flank to await the arrival of the remainder of the squadron from Azizieh. About 11 a.m. the 13th Hussars, near Lajj, suddenly sighted the enemy through the thick mist at close range; in the buffeting wind it was difficult to see or hear, but Colonel Richardson led his regiment in at a gallop and got home with the sabre.

The hussars, however, encountered a devastating fire from a second line, and being unable to locate the flank of the position, held a *nullah* all day under heavy shell and machine-gun fire, at the cost of nine officers and eighty-five men. Both Colonel Richardson and his second in command, Major Twist, were wounded. The Turks evacuated the position during the night.

Two Martinsydes had been caught by a squall and crashed on landing at Zeur. It was unfortunate, as the nearest spare machine was far away at Amara, and we were some distance from the river, without mechanics or protective troops. Before nightfall we had man-handled the aeroplanes across rough country to within the outpost lines by the river. The storm blew throughout the next day. The road was particularly sandy, and the army marched enveloped and choked by solid clouds of sand. It was a following wind, and as it became stirred up the dust floated forward with troops and wagons.

To keep in touch with the troops I accompanied the 3rd Corps in my Hupmobile car; the G.H.Q. ship would be out of touch till nightfall owing to the extraordinarily tortuous course of the river. I shall never forget that ride forward with the column. The ground was intersected by *nullahs* and cut up by the columns in front. Jammed in by guns and transport, it was impossible to move forward at more than five miles an hour; it was almost dark with the intensity of the driving sand, and one could see only a few yards in front when occasionally one opened one's eyes for fleeting glances. Native troops could not be distinguished from British, the grey dust made all men alike. Spread out in marching echelons, with heads muffled up as if in the Arctic regions, the army stumbled on in the gale.

The enemy in Baghdad must have watched with misgiving the vast cloud rolling on. The rapidity of the advance prevented his making a stand in a carefully prepared position and fighting another battle at Ctesiphon, for the cavalry were hard on his heels and reconnoitred to within three miles of the Diala during the day. One pilot carried out a useful reconnaissance in the gale, and reported to Cavalry and 13th Division Headquarters. I managed to get across the river with this report and intercept the G.H.Q. ship, which hauled into the bank.

The 3rd Corps and cavalry division bivouacked for the night of the 6th March about Bustan, having marched seventeen miles. P.S. 53, with General Headquarters, also arrived. General Maude was giving his troops a lead in the front line, and no tired unit felt inclined to lie down when they saw the mast and funnel of the vessel steaming up river ahead of them.

We were close to the ruins of Ctesiphon. This gigantic work of ancient man was the only landmark in the flat treeless waste. From within its arch the Parthian Kings had ruled over their dominions two thousand years ago. Since then, Romans, Arabs, Turks, and British had fought and fallen outside its walls over man's everlasting lust for sovereignty.

The squadron, protected by a company of infantry, remained at Zeur over the 6th and 7th March, repairing one of the crashed Martinsydes and dismantling the other for despatch down river to Busrah.

General Maude put forward the proposition that as no doubt the enemy were evacuating their heavy stores and guns from Baghdad to Samarra by the railway, the interruption of that line might have far-reaching results. So on the 7th two specially selected Engineer officers, Captains Cave-Brown and Farley, with charges of dynamite, left the ground piloted by Lieutenants Windsor and Morris. They managed to land within 200 yards of a railway culvert and kept their engines running. An Arab village lay about 800 yards away, and as soon as the R.E. officers got out of the machines Arab horsemen came galloping down on them. They bolted half-way to gain the culvert, but seeing that the game was obviously impossible, and also realising that their charges were insufficient to wreck the structure, they turned and ran back to the aeroplanes under fire from the Arabs. Both pilots, with their Lewis guns firing, took off straight into the enemy and got away. It was a near shave to losing the lot.

I went on with G.H.Q. in the P.S. 53 up river to Bawi, and

we tied up to the bank on the afternoon of the 7th. The gunboats were just ahead and the 3rd Corps streaming past. Soon after we arrived there was a terrific explosion, and the ship was showered with debris. An ammunition limber had exploded in the middle of a column, and bits of mules and men lay scattered on the bank. We had just succeeded in pulling many live men clear of the shambles, and were cutting some mules adrift, when a bombardier, seeing another limber smouldering, called out to get clear. Hardly a moment elapsed before there was another ear-splitting crash, and some more mules were blown sky-high. It was a sorry job going round with a revolver and shooting these poor mutilated animals.

Our artillery and gunboats were engaging the enemy guns on the other side of the Diala, so I ran on in my motor-launch to the *Mantis*, and joined Buxton in action. His bow six-inch was firing at long range, and we sat on "monkey island" spotting the bursts through our glasses. The Turkish guns were ranging inaccurately, their shells merely sending up great columns of water in the river some way ahead. It was a pleasant spring evening's entertainment, and hard to realise that we were in action, and that the Turkish shells were not part of a "show." Unfortunately a stray enemy shell burst in the midst of a party watering their horses on the bank; a few more would mourn in distant homes.

The squadron landed at Bawi and Bustan, their barges "chugging" on upstream after them. An enemy aeroplane, the first we had seen for many days, hummed round to take note of our dispositions.

That night of the 7th, the King's Own, rowed by volunteers from the rest of the Lancashire Brigade, made an attempt to cross the Diala. Before the first pontoon had been launched every man was shot down; the second got out into the stream, when all its fifteen occupants were killed and the pontoon drifted down the Tigris; the third was blown up by a bomb and sank with all hands; a similar fate attended the fourth and the fifth from a withering machine-gun fire. Next morning the pontoons floating down past us with their cargoes of dead spoke of the deeds of the night. The Lancashire men had not abandoned the attempt till all their five pontoons had gone and their glorious comrades with them.

On the 8th the aeroplanes were busy fixing the exact enemy dispositions in front of Baghdad. The Diala seemed well defended, and on the right bank of the Tigris they were in position some six miles S.S.W. of the city. A pontoon bridge was therefore thrown across the river just south of Bawi and the 1st Corps and cavalry crossed. Some of the 3rd Corps were ferried over higher up to enfilade the Diala position. On the night of the 8/9th, after an intense bombardment, the Loyal North Lancashires dashed for the Diala, and while the smoke of the barrage had yet to clear they gained a footing on the other side; but the party who launched out to support them after the air had cleared, were blown to bits by machine-guns, and the seventy men of Lancashire were left isolated on the north side of the river. With their backs to the Diala they occupied a loop in the recently dug river bund and resisted attack after attack for two nights and a day. Intermittent artillery fire was maintained to support the grand resistance of this gallant band.

Although within shouting distance of our troops on the south side, an attempt by rocket failed to get a cable across for ferrying ammunition. The next night a swimmer half-way over with a line was forced to return, the officer paying out the inshore end being killed. They fought at the point of the bayonet all through the second night, and forty survivors, exhausted and reduced almost to their last cartridge, kept the Turks at bay till rescued at daylight on the 10th. More than a hundred enemy dead were counted lying round the parapet. The story of the passage of the Diala will go down to posterity with the landing at Gallipoli, for the shores at both places are hallowed by the blood of Lancashire. A crossing higher up the river was effected during the night of the 9th by the Wiltshires and East Lancashires. Enfiladed from the opposite bank of the Tigris, and with his left flank turned, the enemy fell back.

Two motor barges loaded with infantry had also gone up river during the night in order to make a landing above the Diala and take the enemy in the rear; but they ran on a shoal, and never reached their destination. I was lying asleep on the deck of P.S. 53 when this disconcerting news came in. Staff officers were routed out, and General Maude awakened from his short sleep. The navy took the situation in hand, and Sherbrooke, of the *Tarantula*, went up river full speed to the rescue. They were towed off just before the: dawn which would have put them at the mercy of the Turkish guns.

During the 9th aeroplanes dropped forty-seven bombs on the railway station, aerodrome, and hostile troops. D. H. blew the roof off the station and destroyed a train at Khazimain with a sixty-five pound bomb. The 1st Corps and cavalry engaged the enemy S.W. of Baghdad, and drove him out of his first position; the cavalry advancing again were saved from walking into an unsuspected second. line by a timely report from the air. The Turks held this second position till nightfall, and caused heavy casualties to our troops by enfilade fire from the other side of the river; his right flank extended far into the desert, and the cavalry were unable to turn it owing to exhaustion and the necessity of returning to the river to water their horses. The high wind and dust storm still prevailed, and the "sea "running in reaches of the Tigris made the "Fly" boats roll heavily and small boat work exciting even in a high-powered Thornycroft launch.

There was no doubt that the enemy had given up all hope of saving Baghdad, and that the strong resistances on the 9th and 10th were merely delaying actions in order to get as many of his stores away as possible. Three weeks before it had never entered the thoughts of men that the British Army would advance so far. Yet here we were hammering at the gates of the City of the Arabian Nights, which for two years had been a mere dream to the expedition on the Tigris. In the history of wars there can never have been an army whose morale was at a higher pitch. Though tired and hungry with the long marches, short rations and incessant fighting, units vied with each other in feats of endurance in their relentless pursuit of the Turk. Commanders were sorely tried to keep their men in check; they would not wait for their rations to come up; they would not sleep; the date-groves and minarets of Baghdad were in sight; they begged to go slap in with the bayonet, and forever add to the annals of their regiment the honour of being the first British troops to arrive.

On the 10th the dust storm, which had lasted for five days, reached its height. Flying in the gale was exciting, but we maintained aerial co-operation throughout the day; the enthusiasm of the men in the air rivalled that of the army on the ground. On the right bank the enemy had evacuated his position and occupied a line of trenches in front of the iron bridge which carried a light railway over a canal two miles south of Baghdad. In the blinding dust it was impossible to see what was taking place or for the artillery to observe targets. The 7th Division suffered heavily through the day; the enemy had the ground well registered and blazed away his ammunition regardless of cost, for they could not take it away with them. On the left bank of the Tigris the 3rd Corps crossed the Diala, which had been bridged by the afternoon. Two miles further north they came up against the enemy's last position in front of Baghdad, the Tel Muhammed ridge. One brigade made a wide flanking movement, and two brigades held him frontally, but he evacuated after dark, and touch was lost in the storm.

The red glow over the city told of flames fanned by the gale; one wondered what was happening in the bazaars that night. At the last conquest of Baghdad, in 1638, the Sultan Murad IV. had put the Persians to the sword, and the conquering army indulged in murder, robbery, and rape; the present inhabitants no doubt expected a similar fate.

By 2 a.m. patrols on the right bank found the Iron Bridge position evacuated. The Black Watch skirmished forward, and with few casualties the 73rd, lean with hunger, fighting, and lack of sleep, went like the wind for Baghdad Railway Station, which they seized at 5.45 a.m., 11th March. On the other bank the Herts Yeomanry and 32nd Lancers rode into the town very soon afterwards.

The Turks, under cover of the darkness and dust storm, had gone hard during the night. At daybreak the aeroplanes were keeping touch with our troops on either bank and reporting by message bag. During the morning two machines landed on the German aerodrome. The gunboat flotilla at Bawi weighed early and proceeded up stream sweeping for mines. The recaptured *Firefly*, with the white ensign over the star and crescent, steamed in the van, again under the command of Lieutenant Eddis, R.N., who had lost her in the retreat from Ctesiphon fifteen months previously. Eddis was under orders for the North Sea, but there was time for him to carry out this last service in Mesopotamia, perhaps the proudest moment of his life and probably unique in the annals of the Royal Navy.

I accompanied Lieutenant Webster in the *Snakefly*. The P.S. 53 with General Maude followed the flotilla. The morning was fine, the dust storm had subsided, and steaming past the palm groves and gardens seemed like entering another world after the long months of strife in the desert. The enemy had endeavoured to bar our passage by placing a heavy chain across the river, but had apparently been too hard pressed to complete the operation, for only one end was made fast.

As we neared the city I went on board the P.S. 53; an aeroplane came gliding down evidently to drop a message on the bank close by, The General Staff had had no reports since weighing anchor, and much importance was attached to the approach of the machine; Chocolo and I stood by betting on the accuracy of the pilot with his message bag. It went into the river and sank like a stone! A wild dash in my motor-boat failed to save it. The breathless staff as the machine approached; the almost exaggerated importance attached thereto; the urgency of picking up the bag at once; the hopeless shot by the 2nd Lieutenant in the air, now speeding away unknowing to his aerodrome; it would have been indecorous to laugh.

We gathered on deck with General Maude as the P.S. 53 rounded the bend into the straight reach of the river that divides the city of Baghdad. The banks were crowded with inhabitants, who had come out in their gala dresses and were waving or solemnly holding white flags. One wondered what General Maude was feeling in this great hour of his success, and felt glad to be there at his side. It had been the achievement of the individual; a student of his profession; a man of iron character and determination; and, above all, of a gentle human being with the love of his troops behind him.

We tied up alongside the old British Residency, now used as a Turkish hospital. Close by was the neutral American Consulate, with the "Stars and Stripes" floating over the roof. I went ashore with O'Riordan, the doctor; we could hardly enter the hospital, the stench was so strong. We walked from bed to bed and looked at the occupants; some were dead and some were alive; some were crawling about on the floor unable to walk. Of sanitary arrangements there were none. For the last few days no attention could have been paid to these wounded and diseased men; most of the wounds had gone to gangrene.

One little Armenian girl, about fourteen years old, was bringing them water; this gallant little soul had been a godmother to the wretched men since the Turkish medical staff had packed up and left them to their fate. It was good to get out into the sunshine and take a breath of God's fresh air again. I crossed the river to the aerodrome situated between the railway station and the German wireless station. This high-powered wireless station had only just been completed a few days as a link in the chain of communication between Berlin and Dar-es-Salaam in German East Africa. They had wrecked it utterly the roof was blown off the main building; the plant within was destroyed; sticks of dynamite were found everywhere. The masts and aerials were buckled up on the ground. Pictures of Zeppelins bombing London and U-boats sinking battleships were splashed with paint on the walls, notably one of the sinking of the *Lusitania*, with the name written large underneath it.

The railway shed was not so completely damaged, but the locomotives were mostly wrecked, having had their cylinders, etc.,

CTESIPHON

GUNBOATS APPROACHING BAGHDAD MARCH 11TH, 1917

blown off by dynamite. The turntable outside the engine-house had been neatly put out of action by one of our bombing aeroplanes. Everything was German; a vast amount of money must have been spent on the place, for it was necessary to import each steel member from Europe and ship them up the Tigris in barges; one realised the death-blow we had dealt to Prussian plans in the Middle East.

On the aerodrome lay the remains of an Albatross, a legacy from the German pilots; on one wing was painted, "With kind regards to our British comrades; the German airmen"; on the fuselage they had written "God Save the King."

A party of Arabs sat nonchalantly squatting in a corner surrounded by Tommies with fixed bayonets; they had been caught sniping some troopers watering at the river. Strong guards were posted on all approaches to the city, and the main thoroughfares were picketed for the night. The Kurds and Arabs had looted and set fire to the bazaars, and terror reigned in the city after the departure of the Turkish Army. Fortunately the British Force arrived in time to restore order and prevent these freebooters massacring or sacking the town completely.

Aerial reconnaissance located the enemy entrenched fourteen miles north on the right bank of the river; another column had retreated in the direction of Baqubah. The cavalry were at Khazimain, beyond Baghdad, but out of touch with the Turk, and the rest of the army bivouacked about Baghdad.

We thought of the newsboys shouting the news down the Strand and the excitement of our folk far away in England.

CHAPTER 4

Baghdad and Beyond

Think, in this batter'd Caravanserai
Whose Doorways are alternate Night and Day,
How Sultan after Sultan with his Pomp
Abode his Hour or two, and went his way.
　　　　　　　　　　　—Omar.

The original Baghdad was a round city on the west bank of the river, built about 762 A.D. by the Caliph Mansur when under the new Abbasid dynasty the Caliphate was moved from Damascus. Haroun al-Raschid, a grandson of Mansur, built his palace on the east bank, round which East Baghdad sprang up. Then known as the Camp of the Mahdi, it was surrounded by a semicircular wall, with its extremities on the river. Traversing Baghdad ran the great Khurasan road; it started from the Khurasan Gate of the Round City and crossed the bridge of boats to East Baghdad, which it left by the second Khurasan Gate.

This caravan road went East through Persia, uniting the capital of the Moslem Empire with its frontier towns on the borders of China. Another road started from the bridge and went North, through the Baradan Gate of East Baghdad, to Samarra and the towns of Northern Mesopotamia. From the Kufa Gate of the Round City started two roads; one West to the towns up the Euphrates, and the other South, the Pilgrim Road to Kufa and Mecca. With the death of Haroun al-Raschid civil war broke out, and in 836 the seat of the Caliphate was moved to Samarra, returning in 892 to East Baghdad. The next five centuries saw the ruin of the Round City.

The plan of Baghdad altered considerably: the new palaces of the Caliphs were built downstream from those occupied by Haroun al-Raschid, and the town extended further to the south; in 1095 another wall was built round the city, the northern portion of which had fallen into ruin. This wall failed to withstand the attack of Hulaku and his Mongol hordes when the Caliphate was wiped out in 1258, but its ruins still encircle modern Baghdad. Timur, a Prince from Turkestan, took the city in 1393, and a Turcoman dynasty reigned over Mesopotamia until the 16th century, when they were rejected by the Persians under Shah Ismail. In 1638, after a long siege, Baghdad fell to the Sultan Murad IV., and Mesopotamia has ever since remained under Ottoman rule.

There are no traces left of the glories of the Round City from which the Caliphs Mansur and Haroun al-Raschid ruled an Empire that extended from China in the East to Spain in the West. It was built entirely of tiles and mud, there being no wood or stone in the country. The modern Baghdad, situated within the ruins of the wall built in 1095, extends also on the west side of the river where the Round City once stood. Beyond the present wall only shapeless mounds and loose bricks indicate the site of ancient buildings.

The two sects of Mahommedans of the Modern Baghdad live in separate quarters of the city. The Shiahs form the entire population of West Baghdad, where they worship at and jealously guard Khazimain, the burial place of two of their recognised descendants of the Prophet, and one of the most important Shiah shrines. The spot is so sacred that no Christian is allowed to set foot therein.

The Sunnis, in the Eastern town, have another almost equally important shrine, but from the point of view of beauty much inferior to the magnificence of Khazimain. Thus the Mahommedan sepoy, be he Shiah or Sunni, besides winning the admiration of his kin had also performed a sacred pilgrimage by the capture of Baghdad. Most of the public buildings are quite modern. The Custom House is built, however, on the same spot as the Medresh of Mostansir, an old college of which only a minaret and a portion of the outer wall, dating from the thirteenth century, remain. The oldest and most picturesque building is the tomb of Zobaida, granddaughter of the Caliph Mansur and wife of Haroun al-Raschid. One of the four great Jewish shrines is Nabi Yusha, the grave of Joshua on the west side of the river; here the Jews bury their high priests.

There were those who, imbued with visions of the days of the Arabian Nights, professed themselves disappointed in the realisation of their expectations. But after a journey through hundreds of miles of desert, the sight of this remote city seemed to me a sufficient fulfilment. Blue-tiled mosques and tall minarets rising above a mass of mud-brick houses, in the distance the golden dome of Khazimain flashing like a flame out of the green of the date groves, and the river winding through all: surely a picture of Romance in its setting of limitless desert.

Few Englishmen had been to Baghdad before the war. The Ottoman Government offered no facilities, and the arrival of strangers was discountenanced; any foreign inquisitors or attempts to develop the trade and resources of the country were jealously guarded against. For the two hundred and eighty years since the Persians had been expelled the district had been governed by intrigue. History has yet to show us that the Asiatic races can hold responsibility without becoming corrupt.

It would seem that the day of Democracy East of Europe is still, in spite of President Wilson and our class agitators, far distant. The germ of unrest fostered in the West since the upheaval of nations has sown disease in the East; there it becomes the code of every man for himself; the benefits of a fair administration by English gentlemen are forgotten and spurned. Agitators rise up and preach sedition to uneducated masses, of whom only a few can read or write.

The loyal English official carries on bravely in his endeavour to stem a tide ever accelerated by the sayings at Westminster;

opinions and rulings of Empire decreed by the votes of inexperienced boys, women or men whose horizon is too frequently bounded by the chimney-pots of their constituencies.

The arrival of the British Army was welcomed by the majority of the population of Baghdad. The only class who resented the invasion were those who held positions of civic importance under the Turk and who bled the poor man white before fulfilling their duties. The chain of corruption started in Stamboul and ended with the Arab beggar in the bazaar. The Departmental head in Stamboul would expect an annuity from his lieutenant in Baghdad. If the latter would retain his position he must raise the necessary amount and as much surplus as possible from his juniors, who, in their turn, exacted it from the poor, who as a result for ever remained starving and downtrodden.

The educated Armenian and Jewish classes hailed us with delight. They knew that the arrival of Englishmen meant fair play, and that their womenfolk would be freed from an everlasting peril. It had been dangerous for the Armenian and Circassian women to walk abroad. A Turkish officer might be attracted by the appearance of a Christian woman in the street, and she, under pain of being put in the public hospital by the health officer as diseased, must needs surrender herself for the satisfaction of the Turk.

Within a few days of our occupation they had cast off their veils and sombre clothing and appeared in bright European creations reminiscent of the accumulations in a Whitechapel emporium. The Baghdad fashions did not entail support for a lady's stockings, generally of multicoloured wool, they invariably hung festooned about the wearer's ankles. The women wore no headgear, but usually possessed a finely-woven cloak of gorgeous colours, known as an *abba*.

Like all foreign towns the place smelt abominably; of sanitary or scavenging arrangements there were none, save the hundreds of diseased and hungry dogs that slunk about the streets in search of offal. The outskirts of the town were a sea of graveyards, and the Mahommedan only buries his relatives beneath a few inches of sand. The sickly smell of decaying humans reminded one of "No Man's Land" in France. Dying animals were taken outside the walls to expire and putrefy. I rode round the outside of the town and felt very sick; the carcases of dogs, mules, horses, donkeys littered the ground. Hundreds of vultures hovered overhead or waddled away too gorged to fly; living dog lay in heavy slumber by the remains of dog half-eaten. In the midst of this charnel-house quadrupeds with ribs sticking through the skin shambled about on their last legs, witnesses of the horror that awaited them. The stench was terrible; my little Arab pony quivered with fright; and, over all, the sun beat mercilessly down.

A group of Armenian girls, survivors of the massacres in the North, were found huddled together in a church. There were few Armenian men in Baghdad, they had all been done to death, and only a handful of girl survivors had drifted South and been taken into Baghdad families or appropriated by Bedouins in the desert. Their tales of the terror that had overtaken them a year before seemed hardly credible in this modern world. One of these girls, whom I met later, gave me a vivid description of how she had hidden in the cupboard of her room while the Turkish soldiers outside put her family and relations to the sword. They belonged to the upper classes, and had only been a short time in Asia Minor after many years in Paris.

It must have been strange to many of the inhabitants of the city that the conquering British Army did not immediately engage itself in wholesale looting, massacre, and rape. Instead, the Baghdadi gaped open-mouthed at the trooper from the Home Counties or the Jock from Dundee, who, after many weeks' marching and fighting, offered him his last cigarette and carried on strange conversation with the dirty little Arab urchins playing in the gutter. The heart of the British Tommy ever shines as a pure bright spot in the blackness of strife, for hatred has no place therein.

A feature that will not be forgotten by many a British Tommy that first day in Baghdad were the oranges; for neither fresh fruit nor vegetables had we tasted for many months. Generals or privates could bury their faces in cool, fresh oranges. I can remember the delight of it now.

For the first few days the inhabitants kept mostly to their houses. The bazaars were shuttered and deserted; many of the shops had been gutted by fire and looted by Kurds. A house-to-house search was instituted and a proclamation issued to the inhabitants to deliver up all arms within a certain date under penalty of death. They were ordered to be in their houses by 6 p.m., for there were 200,000 people of various races to control, and who could tell what might be maturing in the byways of this strange city? The second morning the head of a sepoy was found lying in the gutter; those were days when one walked about armed and in pairs, and kept only to the main thorough-fares in Baghdad.

Rigid police regulations were instituted, a military governor was appointed, and gradually control became established in all quarters of the city. A firm hand was placed over the lawless elements, two gallows were erected in the square, and quickly, quietly, in the early morning those convicted would go to their doom in front of their fellow citizens, who soon learnt the ad-visability of paying heed to the law of the Englishman.

Except for Headquarter units, few of the army had any op-portunity of seeing Baghdad; on the night of the 11th March they bivouacked in its precincts, but marched at dawn in pursuit of the Turkish army, and those who died for their country in the battles beyond, in spite of the consummation of their desires, never saw it at all.

After the occupation of Baghdad the enemy divided into three separate forces, retreating up the Euphrates, Tigris, and Diala rivers. Owing to these scattered dispositions and their dis-tance from Baghdad the General Staff had to rely entirely upon aeroplanes for obtaining quick and accurate information. This entailed long-distance flights over new country, with very inac-curate maps, pilots frequently having to work on a map-scale of 1/2,000,000. The squadron headquarters was 500 miles by river from its base at Busrah, and the ever-prevailing difficulties of transport were doubled. The advanced store barge was moved up from Amara to Sheikh Saad, in order to be halfway between base and front, and the detachment at Nasiriyeh was ordered up to Baghdad to reinforce the somewhat depleted squadron.

Our position at Baghdad could not be secure with the enemy in such close proximity; on any of the three fronts he might be reinforced and descend on the city. There was also the greater danger that he might cut the bunds on the Tigris and Euphrates, thus flood the country with the coming heavy rise in the rivers, and isolate the British Army. The Euphrates is only forty miles away, and at a few feet higher level than the Tigris. If its waters were freed by the Turk they would pour across to the Tigris by Baghdad. It was also important to capture the railhead at Samarra and deny him the use of the railway with which to threaten us from the North.

It was therefore urgent either to force a decision or to drive the enemy beyond our sphere on these two lines. The 13th Turkish Corps was in Persia facing the Russians endeavouring to advance down the Kirmanshah-Karind road. It was also important that these Turks should be prevented from joining the column retreating up the Diala. As the hot weather was approaching, only a few weeks remained in which active operations were practicable, and in order to deal with the above situation the British force could be allowed no breathing space.

On the 12th March aerial reconnaissance discovered the Turkish rearguard in position on the Baghdad-Samarra railway about Mushaidie. On the Euphrates a small enemy force was at Felujah, forty miles west of Baghdad, and on the Diala they occupied Baqubah, thirty-five miles to the north-east. The 3rd Corps kept to the left bank of the Tigris and the 1st Corps to the right. A brigade of the 13th Division marched up the left bank to secure the *bunds*, while the 7th Division, with the 6th Cavalry Brigade, marched north up the railway. On the 13th there was a ground mist and rain, but reconnaissance was carried out.

The gunboats steamed north, and at midnight the 7th Division and 6th Cavalry Brigade advanced on the Mushaidie position. This ran west from the river to the railway, some seven miles inland. The right flank rested among sandhills just west of the line, while between the river and the railway the position was dominated by two mounds and linked by trenches and *nullahs*. Behind, the undulating ground was to the advantage of the enemy; in front we had to attack over bare plain. The Turk must have expected us to advance up the river, as it was here that his guns and men were concentrated. General Cobbe decided to attack the right flank on the railway and turn the position.

At about 4 p.m., after sixteen hours' marching, the Black Watch and 8th Gurkhas deployed and skirmished forward. The enemy fell back on to his second line among the sandhills, but caught our men with a heavy enfilade fire from a mound known as "Sugar Loaf Hill" on his extreme right. The 73rd lost half their officers and the Gurkhas all of theirs but one. The cavalry, far out on the left, co-operated with an enfilade fire, while gunboats bombarded from the river. The right of the Black Watch and the left of the 56th Rifles charged with the bayonet and captured the advanced trenches of the main position. The guns were brought up and under a heavy barrage the Gurkhas and Black Watch carried the second line at 6.30 p.m. At midnight the enemy made a last stand at Mushaidie station, but were rushed by Highlanders and Gurkhas, and fled in a disorderly retreat.

Cobbe's column had fought and marched for two nights and a day; the Turkish Army had been routed with heavy casualties, but the men and horses of our column were dead beat, and the Black Watch and Gurkhas sadly thinned out, with few officers left. The aeroplane co-operation with the artillery was difficult on account of the mobile nature of the fight and continual movement of our guns, but targets were sent down, and pilots could land close to H.Q. throughout the action on the "billiard-table" surface of the ground. Not an enemy machine had been seen.

On the 15th March the Turks were in full retreat towards Samarra in the midst of a gale and dust storm. A column of two brigades of the 14th Division, under Major-General Keary, had arrived on the right bank of the Diala opposite Baqubah; and a column, under General Davidson, was ready to move out west to Felujah on the Euphrates.

Our eyes were turned towards the Persian mountains in the north-east. We knew that the Russians were somewhere up among those snows, a hundred and fifty miles away, we knew also that the 13th Turkish Corps was between us and them. There was a possibility that, with the Turkish army facing the Russians, a force from Baghdad might take them in rear before they could extricate themselves. On the night of the 17th/18th March, Keary's column crossed the Diala and surprised Baqubah, capturing some prisoners and stores. Davidson's column commenced their thirty-five mile desert march on Felujah to endeavour to intercept the Turkish force retiring up the Euphrates from the Nasiriyeh area. Our occupation of Baghdad and proximity to the Turkish communications up the Euphrates had relieved the 1 5th Division at Nasiriyeh of all threat from the enemy, whose small force on that line would have to march hard to save themselves.

The enemy was driven out of Felujah on the 19th, and retired up the Euphrates; air reconnaissance the next day reported several thousand retreating up the river beyond Ramadi; it was evident we had missed the party from downstream. The same morning air reconnaissance spotted the first signs of the Turkish Corps at Shahroban, sixty miles north-east of Baghdad; and further long-distance work discovered infantry, guns, and cavalry marching south-west on that place from Kizil Robat. The enemy apparently meant to hold us up in order to allow their main force coming down from the Pai Tak Pass to cross the Diala. To facilitate co-operation with Keary's column a Flight was despatched from Baghdad to Baqubah.

It was a lovely spring day, and the oranges were thick on the trees when I first saw Baqubah, and I remember how intensely pleased I was with the place; the greenest spot I had yet seen in this arid land. One seemed to be almost out of Mesopotamia. To get there it was necessary to cross thirty-two miles of flat desert;

about half-way was the village of Khan Beni Saad, consisting of a few mud houses, a Khan (caravan resting house), and the wells, but without tree or cultivation; it was the only watering place between Baghdad and Baqubah, and a halt for the caravans on the old Khurasan road. The Arabs at Baqubah cultivated vegetable and fruit gardens, and there was a forest of date palms, past which ran the blue snow water of the Diala; in summer a mere trickle, in winter it can be a raging torrent, rising and falling between its steep banks as much as twenty feet, according to the rain or melting of snow in the hills. We roamed about revelling in the relief of vegetation.

Another Flight went up the Tigris to Kasirin to be further forward and work direct under the orders of the 3rd Corps. The Flight of Martinsydes remained at Baghdad for long-distance G.H.Q. work in any direction.

Our aeroplanes by this time looked weather beaten and dilapidated; we had had no hangars since the crossing of the Tigris, and the machines had been continually exposed to hot sun, wind, dust, or rain. Engine overhauls were few and far between; it reminded one of the early days in France, when in the winter gales of 1914 it was necessary to pierce the fabric of the planes to empty out the water before embarking on the doubtful undertaking of getting a sodden machine off the muddy ground; when the three-ply wood tore apart in one's hand, and when one gaily staggered out over the German lines with a missing engine in a bunch of tricks that would not climb and barely steer.

The demands of each column for continual aerial observation, regardless of the necessary limit to the revolutions of an engine, became impossible to meet. Under central control during the fighting for Kut and the advance on Baghdad it had been possible to co-ordinate work, avoid duplication, and in spite of the heavy demands keep engine overhauls fairly up to date. Before, there had been one front; now there were three. Machines were now detached and decentralised under the command of junior officers at the mercy of any staff officer of the formation with which they were working. Aeroplanes were a new toy to many of the staffs, who sometimes possessed little idea of the first principles of their use or how to work them efficiently, economically, or to full advantage. An occasional remonstrance by a young flight-commander would be squashed by elders and "betters," who knew no more of flying than watching the kites circling over their cantonments in India. Such situations were murderous to effectual co-operation, the efficiency of which hangs on one thread alone, and that of perfect confidence, understanding, and friendship between the two arms.

Once the seed of mistrust or enmity is sown co-operation is over, and no staff bigotry or red tape discipline, but only a resumption of harmony, can ever restore its efficiency. To an air commander such situations are ticklish; fortunately with Force D they seldom occurred. The formation commanders were, above all, human, broad-minded men, and with their help it was soon possible to destroy discord ere it matured. I well remember the only real instance of discord: a Flight which had flown perhaps more than any individual Flight in the war, whose men and material were worn but who still worked at full power with glorious enthusiasm, and who in my opinion possessed the efficiency of veterans, had fallen foul of a certain staff officer, who attempted to dictate beyond his own sphere.

I was thirty miles away, but by telegraphic reports knew that all was not well, and eventually complaints arrived through official channels. Some sort of immediate action was necessary, so I flew out, and sitting on the ground with an unusually morose crowd we hammered the matter out from A to Z. Inelegantly received by the officer in question, little to improve matters was accomplished by arbitration, and to seek an interview and the advice of General Maude was the only course left open. The extraordinarily wide outlook and sense of feeling of the G.O.C. for both sides of a question helped us out of the dilemma, and action was taken to restore what had been lost.

On the 22nd March information came through that the Russians were expected near Khanikin in two days' time, but a reconnaissance which went beyond Kasr-i-Shirin found no trace of them. Keary's column meanwhile pressed the Turks towards Shahroban, which was occupied on the 23rd. Keary was now sixty miles from Baghdad. The cavalry division advanced across the desert from the east bank of the Tigris to co-operate with Keary on the Diala. The country is flat, but broken up by watercuts and *nullahs*; Shahroban is surrounded by cultivation.

To the north-east the long range of barren hills, known as the Jebel Hamrin, runs N.W. and S.E.; from them the waters of the Diala disgorge on to the Mesopotamian plain; and the rough caravan track which was the old Khurasan road winds away over the summit of the hills to the recesses of Persia. From the flat country round Shahroban these low hills, only three or four hundred feet above sea-level, seemed to dominate everything; but in the early morning, before the haze and mirage of the day had obliterated distance, one's eye was tantalised by the snows of the great Persian ranges behind. It was in this low but dominating range that the enemy, reinforced by the advanced troops of the 13th Corps from Persia, took up his position. It was necessary to endeavour to pin him to his ground till the Russians arrived.

So on the night of the 23rd General Keary's two brigades moved forward with the intention of attacking at dawn; they were, however, held up by the numerous canals which had to be bridged. Material was brought up, and the sappers completed their operations on the night of the 24th. By dawn of the 25th, Gurkhas, Dorsets, and Mahrattas of the 9th Brigade were lying down a few hundred yards from the position waiting to attack. The intention was that the 9th Brigade should crush the Turkish left flank against the Diala, when the 8th Brigade would be thrown in frontally.[1]

But the enemy, reinforced from Khanikin, were in too great strength as regards men, guns, and position, and he had the ground and bridge sites accurately ranged. After driving in his outposts our troops were held up by a withering fire from the

---

1. See map.

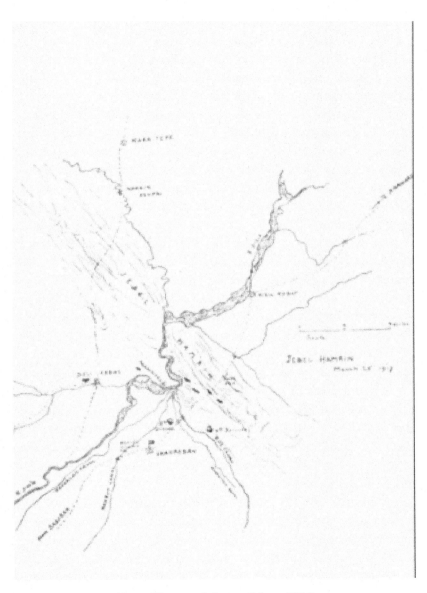

JEBEL HAMRIN, MARCH 25TH, 1917

broken ground above them, and in the mass of hills it was difficult to locate the Turkish guns, which in any case were well protected against our shells by the contour of the ground. In the heat of the day heavy counter-attacks were launched, and, our flanks being in danger of envelopment, a general retirement was ordered. The Turkish cavalry attempted to charge, but were mowed down by steady rifle and machine-gun fire.

The British Force, having lost a thousand casualties, eventually regained and consolidated a line along the Ruz Canal. The enemy's strong position in the Jebel Hamrin now ensured the safe passage of their 13th Corps across the Diala, and it soon became evident that, far from contemplating retirement towards Kifri, they intended effecting a junction with their 18th Corps on the Tigris.

On the Euphrates the Turkish Force were observed retiring beyond Ramadi; on the Tigris aerial reconnaissance detected a trench system being dug at Istabulat to cover Samarra. The aeroplanes were humming on all three lines. The co-ordination of work with three forces; difficulties of supply far out in the desert; direction of river, motor, and mule transport; supervision of the Aircraft Park, five hundred miles downstream; and the estimating six months ahead for stores from England; these were only a few of the mass of subjects to be dealt with. Chocolo, Huxley, Somers-Clarke, and myself were on all fronts during the day, and pored over our maps and papers far into the night. Enemy machines were now occasionally seen, and reliable intelligence kept sifting through that twelve more were soon expected, some of them Halberstadts.

As regards supplies he was on interior lines, which enabled him to introduce a new type of machine at the front at least a fortnight sooner than we could. In view of his remarkable inferiority in the air during the past months, it was inevitable that he would try and wrest our supremacy from us by springing some surprise. Cables fully representing the danger to which we were exposed had been repeatedly despatched to London. The obsolete B.E., Martinsyde, and old Bristol Scouts were quite inadequate to cope with the possible arrival of the machines which were closely combating our fastest scouts in France. *Via* Cairo, or perhaps even London, reports caught in the web of a great intelligence system percolated back to Baghdad: 200 German flying personnel had been seen at Vienna, dressed as for a hot climate; a week later Cairo would cable that aeroplanes in packing-cases had been seen on the railway station at Constantinople; yet again our own agents would report these packing cases at Ras el Ain, on the Baghdad railway; and so the story wove itself into fact. At last the Air Board in London were able to promise us new machines. "Spads," a fast-fighting type, were being sent from England; but they would not be in time.

East of the Diala General Keary contained the Turkish force in the Jebel Hamrin. On the west the enemy commenced a converging movement: part of the 13th Corps down through Deli Abbas and part of the 18th Corps across the Adhaim River along the left bank of the Tigris. I took a machine out to have a look at this movement, and could see the long Turkish columns winding like black snakes against the colourless contours of the Jebel Hamrin. They stopped on sighting my aeroplane, and several parties commenced to walk back in the opposite direction, but their intention was too obvious.

On the 27th the cavalry division resisted the enemy's forward movement on the west bank of the Diala about Deltawa, and forced him back towards Deli Abbas on the following day. On the night of the 28th, the 39th and 40th Brigades of the 13th Division deployed to attack the Turkish force that had come down the Tigris, and was entrenched near Dogameh. The advance lay across the dead flat Marl Plain, devoid of the cover of a blade of grass. The enemy's left flank extended so far into the desert that both brigades were forced to attack frontally. The 40th held them on the left while the 39th endeavoured to turn their right.

The weather was hot, and owing to mirage the attack was suspended during the heat of the day. In the evening a determined onslaught drove the Turks out of their position, and they fell back across the Adhaim under cover of darkness. The two brigades had suffered heavily, but our object had been attained; the converging movement had been frustrated by the defeat of both forces in detail. Aerial co-operation with the artillery had proved of great assistance in this action, when intensive artillery support afforded our infantry their sole chance of closing with the Turk.

A curious outstanding feature of the fighting on the flats of Mesopotamia was the medley of artillery observation ladders which sprang up out of the desert whenever the guns went into action. Without them it was quite impossible for a battery commander to see anything at all. They were run up some distance from the batteries as far forward as possible, and invariably acted as a magnet to the enemy gunfire. The utmost gallantry was displayed by gunner officers, who remained perched behind a bullet-proof shield on the top of one of these swaying poles directing the fire, until the smoke and dust around them became too thick to see through, or they were blown off the platform by an accurately-placed "crump."

On the 30th March D. H. went out in search of the Russians with a despatch from General Maude to General Baratoff. He flew over the Persian frontier to Kasr-i-Shirin and beyond, but failed to find any trace of a Cossack. His account of flying a few feet above snow ridges and in among green valleys with rushing mountain streams and wooded slopes made our mouths water, down in the dusty arid plain, where the midday temperature was already touching 100 degrees Fahr. in the shade, and the prospect of another "hot weather" was depressing. The competition to fly out to this cool mountain country and gain the honour of being the first British officer to meet the Russians was keen.

On the 31st the cavalry division occupied Deli Abbas and the Turkish force opposite Keary in the Jebel Hamrin on the left bank of the Diala retired across that river. It was evident that except for perhaps a rear party the whole of the enemy force must now be across and the Russian army not very far away. We heard the next day that Baratoff's advanced guard had reached the Pai

Tak Pass, and were descending towards Kasr-i-Shirin.

Lieutenant Windsor reconnoitred to Hit on the Euphrates 100 miles west of Baghdad, but the enemy on this line had remained quiet. Our troops were in Felujah, with an outpost upstream at Saklawieh. We had not been in time to prevent the Turk from cutting a dam at the latter place, and the water was streaming through the opening into the Akkarkuf Lake, which had flooded over until the water was now lapping against the railway embankment at Baghdad; it sluiced through the channel under the Iron Bridge into the Tigris, but was steadily rising, and as far as the eye could see to the north and west a great sea stretched to the horizon.

On the right bank of the Tigris the enemy occupied Sumaikcheh, and on the left bank was in position behind the Adhaim River. Such were the general dispositions on the 1st April, when the 13th Turkish Corps were retiring on Kifri.

At 6 a.m. on the morning of the 2nd I left Baghdad in a Martinsyde with the despatch that General Maude had been trying to get through to Baratoff, for as yet no meeting had taken place between the Cossacks and the patrols of Keary's column. My course took me straight out across the Jebel Hamrin to Khanikin, and over the Persian foothills to Kasr-i-Shirin. It was a lovely spring day, the country below was green, the air above cool and bracing; how good it felt to be clear of Mesopotamia. Looking back I could just discern the hill country disappearing down to the thick haze of noonday in the desert; looking ahead it seemed I was flying into a great wall of massive peaks, with their snows scintillating in the sunlight above me. I opened my throttle and climbed to 10,000 feet, but only caught a view of further snows beyond. The beauty of it to the eye, wearied by dust and desert, was intoxicating. It was a different world, and the desire was strong to land in one of those remote little glens where one could roll in the grass and bathe in the burn. I had not seen grass for nine long months.

At Kasr-i-Shirin the road turns almost south-east before the long thirty-five mile climb up to the Pai Tak Pass, the gateway from the high plateaux of Persia down to the plains of Mesopotamia. After flying for three hours I spied a column of cavalry on the march, passing a village called Miankul. Not knowing if they were retreating Turks or advancing Russians, I glided slowly down. They made no movement to fire, so I glided on lower and lower till, in answer to my hand-wave, they threw their fur caps in the air; I knew that at last we were in touch with the Russians. I landed on a patch of level ground not far off the road, and they galloped up, solemnly saluted, and shook me by the hand, each in turn. This wild-looking group of Cossacks, clustered around me in their picturesque long coats and sheepskin hats cocked at a rakish angle, against the background of mountain valley and pass winding away up to the rugged snow hills, made a scene I shall not forget. They had come from Caucasia, down past the Caspian to Persia, a march of a thousand miles through uncivilised countries, no lines of communication behind them, and without transport, finding what they could to live on as they went. Their little ponies were skin and bone, they themselves hard and lean, burnt black by the sun in striking contrast to their blue eyes and fair moustaches. Two or three junior officers were there, but not a word of any language had we in common. The despatch they understood, and I pointed up the pass and said "Baratoff." I had left my engine just ticking over, and having only sufficient petrol to take me straight back to Baghdad could spare no further time; once stopped, the problem of starting again was too uncertain. They each saluted, again shook me by the hand, and as I left the ground gave a weird shout and threw their hats in the air. It had been a dramatic meeting. With regret I dropped back into the Mesopotamian desert from that beautiful mountain region of snow and wild flowers, and after five hours' flying into what had seemed some dream country landed in the relentless heat and glare of Baghdad.

The same morning a small column under Brigadier-General Edwardes, that had pushed out to Kizil Robat, met a *sotnia* of Cossacks who had been sent far on in advance to establish communication with the English army.

The long-expected arrival of new enemy aeroplanes materialised, for they made their début on the following day, April 3rd, when Lieutenants Page and Rattray, reconnoitring up the Tigris, sighted a hostile machine and gave chase. During the pursuit a second hostile machine suddenly dived past Page's machine and came up a hundred yards on the left front. Page veered left-handed to get the enemy to his right so that his forward gun would bear.

But the enemy countered to keep the same side, and Page, intent on not giving an inch, held straight on his course to get to the left. So determined was each pilot to make the other give way that the machines, closing at the rate of 180 miles an hour, collided at the wing tips, which were cut off as if by a knife. The enemy immediately made off north for Samarra, and Page managed to get back to his aerodrome at Kasirin. It is interesting to compare the perverted German wireless news:

> One of the Fokkers, piloted by Captain Schutz, rammed a hostile plane in air-combat and caused it to fall. Our machine brought back a wing torn off the enemy plane and landed safely in our lines.

with our own report:

> The enemy machines appeared to be hit, and, according to tribal report, the larger of the two was compelled to land somewhere on the right bank of the Tigris, and was burnt.

This was confirmed on the 14th April, when the charred remains were discovered by Fane's column. Page, in an old B.E., had put the fear of God into two of the fastest enemy scouts. The flight home with a wing-tip gone and the rest of the plane threatening to carry away must have caused him and Rattray some long and anxious minutes. Page treated this incident in the same light as when, soon after joining us in earlier days at Arab Village, he crawled out of wreckage so complete that only an electric switch was recognisable, and I had nearly given him the sack for grinning. He came from the Yeomanry in Egypt, and he served with us until I had gone, when, alas! this glowing spirit met his end in the desert after eighteen months' continuous flying.

On April 4th orders were issued by the General Staff for further operations on both banks of the Tigris. Our troops concentrated in two columns; that on the left bank under Lieutenant-General Marshall, and that on the right bank under Major-General Fane. The Flight at Baqubah, on the Diala, was transferred to Fort Kermeah, on the Tigris, the riverhead for General Fane's column, and the Flight already on the Tigris at Kasirin moved upstream to Kuwar Reach, the riverhead for General Marshall's column. In view of the menace of fast enemy machines, Aircraft Park at Busrah worked hard to put into commission a few Bristol Scouts that had been sent from Egypt as a stop-gap pending the arrival of the Spads from England.

These Bristols, with their Clerget engines, could not however be considered a match for the Hun Halberstadt. Fortunately, long superiority over the enemy had bred the utmost confidence in our pilots, and we had by this time collected a dauntless gang of cheerful souls quite firmly convinced that they were second to none. The prospect of "scraps" to come acted as a tonic to the gayer spirits in the mess. D. H. flew a worn-out B.E. to Busrah, and was back next morning with a Bristol, having covered the double journey of 750 miles in eight hours' actual flying; Paddy Maguire was *en route* with another.

A captured 100-horse-power German Gnome engine was fitted in a third, and it gave her a fine turn of speed. Unfortunately the extra weight of this engine spoilt the trim of the machine and made her difficult to handle in the air. She eventually stuck her nose into the mud at Amara on the way to the front, and was totally wrecked.

On Easter Sunday, April 8th, Fane's column advanced up the railway and captured Beled station, two hundred prisoners, and some rolling-stock, after a sharp fight with the Turkish rearguard. The next day they occupied Harbe, and halted pending developments on the opposite bank of the Tigris. It had been intended that General Marshall's column should now force the Adhaim and drive the 52nd Turkish Division back on Samarra. On the 9th, however, it became evident that Ihsan Bey with his 13th Corps in the Jebei Hamrin was advancing down through Deli Abbas along the Nahr Khalis Canal towards Deltawa, apparently another effort at effecting a junction with the 52nd Division on the Adhaim.

On this day I left once more with despatches from General Maude to General Baratoff, whose advanced troops had occupied Kasr-i-Shirin, and were picqueted along the line of the Diala above the Jebel Hamrin. The morning was hot, and getting through the first 4,000 feet behind the big Beardmore engine of a Martinsyde scout was as warm a performance as the engine-room watch in a destroyer. However, the prospect of another day among the hills banished all feelings of discomfort in the getting there.

A detour on the way out disclosed the enemy columns winding down on to the plain near Deli Abbas, a long string of crawling ants followed by the white specks of ambulance wagons. It was lovely to get back among these ranges again, but this time my flight only took me as far as Kasr-i-Shirin, 120 miles N.E. of Baghdad, and just over the Persian frontier. I landed on a rough grassy space about a mile outside the town, among the stones which are the ruins of the great Sassanian Palace of Shirin, the mistress of King Parwiz. Bits of this lady's palace were nearly the undoing of my aeroplane, which only by mere luck came to rest on the stony slope without hitting any of these relics of ancient majesty.

Cossacks streamed over a knoll which hid the town from view, and soon some Russian officers, including a colonel, arrived with an escort and spare pony. After much saluting and hand-shaking, I mounted this ragged animal and, leaving sentries to guard the machine, we rode solemnly towards the town. Just outside we came upon the bivouac of an infantry battalion, the guard was turned out in waiting, and to my surprise there was also a brass band. They had no ammunition; they had no food or forage; they had come hundreds of miles over burning desert and ice-bound mountain passes, and through all they had stuck to their brass band!

As we approached it struck up "God Save the King." We dismounted with our hands at the salute; all the verses were played through, and I was about to drop my hand, when the anthem started again. I think they played the National Anthem for ten minutes without stopping; each time the last chords of the refrain were reached I thought it was the end, and I could allow my cramped arm to drop, but immediately the band would start again. At last they could blow no more; the remainder of the battalion and many Cossacks had collected, their colonel made a short speech, raised his hat in the air, and the Russian army gave vent to some wild cheering which necessitated further saluting on my part.

A procession of officers was then formed, and we adjourned to the only tent. It was of single thickness, and the sun's rays had made the atmosphere within like an oven. As many officers as possible wedged themselves in, the colonel and I being the only two who had chairs. So far not a word had been exchanged; I could talk no Russian and they had neither English nor French. So they conversed excitedly together and gaped at me. *Arak* (native spirit) was produced, and with wild acclamation we drank to the health of both nations.

Fortunately Colonel Rowlandson, the British liaison officer with the Russian army, soon rescued me from the appalling atmosphere, and we rode on into Kasr-i-Shirin. There I met the Russian officer in command and handed him the despatch for General Baratoff. The Staff were magnificently dressed in long dark coats, belted and skirted, curved swords and daggers in ivory scabbards, ivory cartridge cases across their breasts, and white sheepskin caps. The valleys were hot enough, but one wondered how they would fare in that kit if they went down into Mesopotamia. The rank and file were ragged, and few of their jackboots had the soles intact; some of them walked about with cloth wrapped round their feet. Kasr-i-Shirin is a pretty little hill village, a mountain stream running past in the glen below; it looked enticingly clean and cool, and the Russian soldiers were bathing in its pools.

We had lunch in the building once occupied by the Indo-Persian Telegraph Company, since wrecked by the Turks. It was an interesting luncheon party; a few of the staff could talk French, and one, I recollect, was a Hungarian who had espoused the Russian cause. Fortunately there was only sufficient *Arak* to go round, and the rest of the drinking was done in tea. *Arak* is a fire water made of raisins; it was the heat of the day, and there was the long flight back to Baghdad in front of me. I was escorted back to the aeroplane, and to the tune of "God Save the King" by that amazing brass band, I waved farewell to my enthusiastic friends and left the ground for Baghdad. After another detour to observe the progress of the 13th Turkish Corps I landed at Fort Kermeah, on the Tigris. The weather had stoked up considerably in the last few days, and it was with difficulty that the water in one's radiator was kept from boiling. Six hours' flying in a Martinsyde left one like a wet rag, and drove me down before reaching Headquarters.

Fort Kermeah was a square mud enclosure with flat desert on all sides, and a quarter of a mile away, screened by its steep banks, flowed the Tigris. Some refreshment and the cheerful meeting with friends was restoring, and I reached Baghdad before nightfall.

Lieutenants Page and Rattray had been interfered with by a Halberstadt while co-operating with the artillery on the Adhaim, but after two drums of ammunition emptied at close range, and under the fire of our A.A. guns, the Hun had turned for Samarra and left our machine to continue its work.

Orders were given for General Fane to hold the enemy about Harbe, and Marshall's column to act offensively against the 13th Turkish Corps advancing from Deli Abbas. On the 10th the cavalry division, who were out on General Marshall's right flank between Deltawa and Deli Abbas, came in contact and fell back in front of the enemy. That evening Captain Bayly and myself took out two Martinsyde scouts loaded with bombs to see if we could break one of the new enemy scouts on the ground at Samarra. We made out to the northward in company, but near Beled I observed Bayly manoeuvring some distance to starboard. I closed to investigate and then spotted that he was engaged with a Hun which was going down on top of him.

I arrived on the scene just as the Halberstadt shot below my level, at 6,500 feet, and there we were, all three shrieking down, one on top of the other, at about 150 miles an hour. I should have settled him with a drum of ammunition, but he was diving in a curve, and the stream of bullets must have just passed by. He pulled out, and we each started climbing for the right side of the sun, which was low and blinding. Bayly had got too low, and was lost to sight. I was carrying two 112 lb. bombs, and immediately tried to release these, which hindered both climbing and manoeuvring.

Unfortunately one bomb jammed and the release gear carried away in my efforts to lighten the machine, so there I was with a heavy list, carrying a 112 lb. dead weight on one side and a fast enemy scout manoeuvring for the *coup de grâce*. The situation was awkward. After a few minutes he turned and came straight at me from above, and cocking the old Martinsyde up on her tail I just got the gun to bear. She lost flying speed, fell sideways, and then nose-dived 1,000 feet before I could regain control. Like a fool he never followed me down, or I should have been "meat," but, climbing higher, disappeared towards his base. It was nearly dark, and I was 100 miles from home. Bayly's machine was badly riddled about the under-carriage, and collapsed on landing. Our evening's expedition had turned out more exciting than had been expected.

The 13th Turkish Corps had halted on the 10th. That night two brigades of Marshall's troops made a twenty-mile march on Ihsan Bey's right flank and met the Turkish troops in the open, endeavouring to outflank our cavalry at dawn on the 11th. It was a surprise action. The 39th and 40th Brigades gained the only commanding slope of ground before the Turks could reach it, and, lying down under the fierce sun, held the enemy while a brigade of Field Artillery galloped to their assistance close up behind the ridge and came into action at close range. The advance was checked, and the Turks, leaving three hundred dead, retired six miles during the night. In the stiff fighting, without a vestige of shade and after their long night march, the 39th and 40th Brigades suffered heavily from heat and lack of water. The men were still in their heavy winter khaki, for the demands on the river transport had not yet allowed for all the summer clothing to be brought upstream.

Aeroplanes had difficulty in running their engines during the heat of the day due to the oil running thin; they were, however, the only means of overcoming the mirage in the desert, ground observation being useless and misleading.

The machines were busy on all fronts. At daybreak on the 12th Captain Bayly and Lieutenant Windsor arrived over the Samarra aerodrome, at 3,400 feet, and obtained a direct hit with a 65 lb. bomb on a hostile biplane. The railway station and rolling stock were also bombed and damaged. The raid was carried out under heavy A.A. and machine-gun fire. The Turks were digging a position across the railway at Istabulat, ten miles south-east of Samarra; twenty-eight gun-pits had been dug. A detachment of the enemy were also seen coming from the Euphrates line at Samarra.

The enemy on the Adhaim were held by a sufficient force of Marshall's column while the main force dealt with Ihsan Bey, who continued his retreat on the 12th, pursued by the cavalry. The Turks fought their usual stubborn and effective rearguard action throughout the 13th and 14th. The cavalry division attempted by a wide detour to get behind them across the Kifri Road, but lack of water and their strong entrenched flank position prevented such achievement. Ihsan Bey got back into the shelter of the Jebel Hamrin during the night of the 14th April.

Heat was beginning to restrict the performance of aeroplanes; we were still flying the old B.E.s, but although obsolete for war purposes, their stationary air-cooled engines were less vulnerable to high temperature than the rotary type in the Bristols or the water-cooled in the Martinsydes. Captain Pickering flew B.E.2C 4500 from the base to Fort Kermeah; she was a veteran machine, having been in action with Townshend at the battle of Ctesiphon in 1915. To maintain ourselves it was necessary to ship any crashed or old machines down to Busrah, where, after being entirely renovated, they were flown back to the Front, and with their old numbers and spirit of past fame they were better than new.

Two Martinsydes which were fitted with special tropical radiators did not overheat as yet, but it was doubtful that they would keep the air throughout the hot weather, and the heat behind the engine in the pilot's seat was already well-nigh unendurable. Those without special radiators were now no use and out of action, as the water boiled away even if flown at dawn. It was a gamble how long the Bristol Scouts would last; they were already coming down with "blued" cylinders, and making forced landings with pistons seized. One only hoped that the Hun was faced with the same problems; if nought but old Ctesiphon B.E.s remained to meet his new productions even our last jokes might fall flat.

The enemy's second attempt at effecting a junction between his 13th and 18th Corps was again frustrated by defeating both detachments in detail. Orders were now issued for Marshall's column to detach the cavalry division and two brigades of infantry to contain the 13th Corps, and with the remainder of troops to make preparations to force the passage of the Adhaim River.

Fane's column on the right bank of the Tigris, which had been absorbed under General Cobbe's command, were to advance towards the Istabulat position. General Maude never ceased harrying the enemy, thus keeping the initiative in his own hands. The scene of battle swung relentlessly from one front to another; the troops had become veterans in desert warfare, and the supply services, 500 miles from their base, had forgotten the meaning of the word impossible.

Every Monday morning it was my fortune to attend a conference at G.H.Q., where the heads of all departments met, plans were disclosed, past events reviewed, and the million problems regarding the maintenance and efficiency of the army were discussed direct with our chief. He knew the duties of his staff directorates down to the smallest detail. They were instructive, those conferences; one learnt of the stone walls other people were up against, and one learnt how, when perhaps an engineering problem was deemed impracticable, the necessity thereof, backed by the humour and method of General Maude, crumbled another stone wall. In that assemblage of staff officers sitting sweltering under the fans, his was a personality dominant and absorbing.

On the 15th Captain Pickering and Lieutenant Craig left at daybreak on reconnaissance for Cobbe's column, but they never returned. A sand storm and gale of wind arose in the morning, which became too violent to send out a search machine; cavalry and armoured cars scoured the country to no account. Later the sad news was received that old B.E. 2C 4500 met her end in a fight with a Halberstadt, and both Pickering and Craig had been killed. The gale continued all the next day, and it was impossible to leave the ground. On the 17th Paddy Maguire arrived with a new Bristol Scout in four hours twenty minutes from Busrah, intent on avenging the deaths of Craig and Pickering.

Aerial photography of the country on all fronts had been pressed on daily. There were no maps, and to fight the Turk without eliminated any chance of the co-operation on which success depended. The photographic section were developing and printing far into each night, and with the results the mapping section at G.H.Q. turned out accurate squared maps which were distributed by air on the front. Often last editions of these, showing the latest enemy earthworks photographed a few hours previously, would be dropped from the air to units just about to attack. The mapping of the Adhaim River had not yet been completed, but Lieutenant Beckett sketched it from its mouth to the Jebel Hamrin; its bed is in places more than a mile wide, a mass of shifting channels and quicksands. The water dries into a few pools in the hot weather.

The crossing was effected during the night of the 17th/18th, again by the Lancashire Brigade, of Diala fame. Two battalions ferried themselves over in the darkness, unsuspected by the enemy, at a point some distance below where another battalion had ostentatiously forded the river; a cavalry brigade, under Colonel Cassels, also demonstrated on the northern flank. The enemy were confused. The main crossing against the Turkish centre was a complete surprise: the cliffs were stormed at the coming of the dawn and the enemy outposts threw down their arms.

The sappers and miners started building a bridge, and the aeroplanes were up there waiting to co-operate with the artillery. The co-operation worked splendidly, and at 12.30 p.m. three Lancashire battalions went in with the bayonet under a drum-fire barrage. The enemy's resistance collapsed, and then Cassels' cavalry, who had been brought in from their feint, drove through between the Turks and the Tigris, cutting them off from water. Those of the enemy who were not killed or wounded threw down their arms; Cassels pursued till nightfall, and hardly a Turk got away. Much of the success of the day was due to the magnificent artillery work. The following is an extract from the artillery report:

All batteries were in action from 4 a.m. onwards. About 6 a.m. H.M.S. *Tarantula* opened fire with six-inch gun, and H.M.S. *Waterfly* with four-inch gun. Observation difficult owing to clouds of dust hanging over enemy position. Three aeroplanes co-operated with the R.A. from 5 a.m. till 10.30 a.m., and from 11.30 a.m. till 1 p.m., using 'smoke balls,' very useful registration being carried out before bombardment at 12.30 p.m. At 12.30 p.m. barrage was put up on Turkish position astride the Narhwan Canal, C and D 55 and 61st Batteries bombarding trenches, 60th Battery *kloofs* on both banks of the canal, and the R.N. and 2/104th Battery the bed of canal in rear of

Turkish position. Duration of bombardment, fifteen minutes. Rates, of fire: 18-pounders, two rounds per gun per minute; 4.5 howitzers and 60-pounders, one round per gun per minute. Parties of retiring Turks were then engaged. At 2 p.m. pursuit had moved out of range of guns, and sections of 'S' R.H.A. and D 66 Batteries accompanied and supported Cassels' Cavalry Brigade. Turkish prisoners report many wounded by our artillery fire.

One thousand three hundred prisoners were taken, and the enemy casualties in killed and wounded were very heavy.

The Flights at Kuwar Reach and Fort Kermeah now moved further upstream to Barurah on the left bank of the river. Aeroplane reconnaissance was mainly confined to early morning and evening on account of the intense heat during the day. Owing to the continual and almost daily movement of Flights, it had been impossible for the last two months to put machines under hangars, and in order to protect them from the sun during the day they were covered with *chattai* (palm-leaf mats).

It afforded good protection, and kept the fabric cool. The main object was to keep the light off the doped fabric; heat had small deteriorating effect compared to the light of the sun's rays. Tent hangars being unable to withstand the frequent violent squalls were useless in that country; they also had no ventilation when closed, and the temperature inside became terrific and destructive to the woodwork. The heavy R.A.F. hangars were of too permanent a nature to keep pace with our movements.

On the 19th the 7th Division took up a position about 3,000 yards from the 18th Turkish Corps at Istabulat. The Adhaim fighting had cleared the left bank, and it was now practicable for General Cobbe to force a decision with Shefket Pasha and drive him behind Samarra, which would give us the entire hundred-mile section of the Baghdad railway.

The enemy occupied a position of great strength at Istabulat, facing S.E., with their left on the river.[1] Their front-line trench-

---

1. See sketch map. overleaf..

es ran along a ridge for two-and-a-half miles to the railway, and then bent back for several miles parallel to it. The Dujail Canal, an ancient irrigation work, cut through the Turkish position and ran S.E. through our own front line. The enemy trenches commanded dead flat ground on all sides, and between the canal and the river his line contained two strong redoubts. This position was held by 6,700 rifles, 200 sabres, and thirty-one guns, whilst in reserve at Samarra he had nearly the same again.

On the 20th April the Turkish advanced posts were driven in, and our attacking troops concentrated in a forward position which had been dug during the night. It was decided to go for the two redoubts first.

At dawn of the 21st the Black Watch and 8th Gurkhas advanced across the plain under cover of a creeping barrage. With dropping casualties the first wave reached the foot of the ridge, from the crest of which the enemy poured a devastating fire. The barrage lifted, and with an irresistible rush they were in with the bayonet. The garrison of the northern redoubt surrendered to the Gurkhas; the Black Watch, after a bloody struggle, drove the Turks from the Dujail, but were forced out again by a violent counter-attack a few minutes later.

The "Hielanders" swept up the slopes once more, and finally held the position against several desperate hand-to-hand counter-attacks in spite of losing more than half their officers. The Seaforths and two battalions of Punjabis now assaulted the line to the south of the canal, and by 7.30 a.m. the whole front trench was in our hands. The 9th Bhopal Infantry, co-operating to the extreme right of the Gurkhas, had come under a cross-fire and been decimated, only one officer surviving.

The aeroplanes co-operated with the artillery in keeping down the fire of the enemy's guns. Lieutenant Lander had a fight with a Halberstadt, and drove him down on to his own aerodrome. The day became very hot, and was spent consolidating what had been gained, and the enemy evacuated his position during the night, retiring to another position six miles from Samarra.

Sketch Showing Battle of Istabulat

On the 22nd a fresh brigade of the 7th Division pressed on in the heat, and were in contact by noon. The position ran along ridges that extended from the river to the railway.[2] The Leicesters and 51st Sikhs advanced towards the Turkish left near the river, while Colonel Cassels' cavalry and armoured cars operated on the desert flank. On the opposite bank of the river a column with guns under General Thompson had marched up from the Adhaim. These guns on the other side of the river took up a position actually behind the flank of the Turkish line. When the bombardment opened at 4 p.m. their effect was deadly. The Turks did not wait for the bayonets of the Leicesters; they bolted across country, but it was too much for our men, who pressed on after them till they were on top of the guns.

A whole battery of seven guns surrendered; the remainder of the Turkish army appeared to be in full flight across the plain. But the Leicesters were out of touch, the enemy rallied and counter-attacked, and the Leicesters, in danger of being overwhelmed, were forced to retire, leaving their captured guns behind. It was only the desperate fighting of the 56th Rifles and 53rd Sikhs that held up this counter-attack and saved the situation. The 32nd Lancers also charged in from the desert flank; they jumped a trench, from which the enemy bolted and was stuck, but, coming under a heavy fire, were driven back with severe casualties. Their colonel and adjutant were killed leading the charge. Shefket Pasha retired, and our troops, exhausted and parched with thirst, halted for the night. They had been fighting and marching all day in a temperature of 110 deg. Fahr. in the shade.

During the fighting Lieutenant Maguire, on patrol in a Bristol Scout, sighted a Halberstadt over Istabulat at 7,500 feet. The two machines closed and fought a duel in full view of the troops on the ground. The enemy had the advantage of the Bristol Scout both in speed and climb, but was outmanoeuvred by Maguire, who, while being dived at, got on to the tail of the Hun by a violent turn and followed down, his Vickers gun going hard.

2. See sketch map.

SAMARRA
NOTE THE TRACINGS OF ANCIENT CITIES ON THE SURROUNDING DESERT

Some part of the hostile machine shot past the top plane of the Bristol, and the Hun seemed to lose control. At 4,000 feet both the wings on one side carried away, and he continued his career like a stone to the earth. Troops nearby heard a whistling shriek as of a heavy shell coming over; then a crash and a cloud of dust, and the ground was littered with the debris of what had once been an aeroplane.

The following telegram was received from Cobbe's column:

Pilot of Turkish machine brought down was a German with fair small moustache, in Turkish uniform, without badges, but bearing No. 39 K.G.A.G. 1915. No name discernible. Death instantaneous. In his pocket was pass for Constantinople for Sergeant Conrad. Engine bore plate 'Argus Flugmotor No. 2263 Berlin Reinichendorff.' Chassis wheels fitted with Continental pneumatic tyres, but filled with asbestos strips, and tyres bound to the wheels by string. All engine fittings wrecked.

Paddy Maguire had defeated his better-mounted opponent only by sheer courage and skill; Pickering and Craig were avenged; the Flying Corps messes sang themselves to bed.

On the early morning of the 23rd April our troops occupied Samaria station. The place had been burnt out, but the enemy had not had time to destroy completely all the rolling-stock or locomotives. During the last three days the following captures had been made: twenty officers (including battalion and battery commanders), 667 other ranks, one Krupp gun, one 5.9 howitzer, two machine-guns, 1,240 rifles, sixteen locomotives (some repairable), 240 trucks (large proportion undamaged), two barges, and many other stores. Turkish losses in killed and wounded were given by prisoners as over 3,700 at Istabulat alone.

While the battle had been raging aerial news came in that the 13th Turkish Corps was once again on the move, and by forced marches was already advancing down the Adhaim from the direction of Kara Tepe. Apparently a forlorn hope to save Samarra. On the evening of the 23rd his leading division occupied a position within touch of Marshall's troops, who were near the junction of the Adhaim and Tigris. But they had outstripped their comrades in rear; their other division was seven miles back. General Marshall, seizing the opportunity of defeating him in detail, marched through the night up the west bank of the Adhaim and bumped into the enemy just before dawn.

The cavalry and one brigade made an enveloping movement to the north, while another brigade attacked frontally, supported by our artillery at only half a mile range. After a short resistance the enemy gave way and fled across the river, affording grand shooting for our guns, which accounted for 100 crumpled Turks. The British troops found what shade they could through the day, and that evening air reconnaissance reported the enemy retiring up both banks of the Adhaim. Marshall's column followed up through the night.

On the evening of the 25th a line of defence was observed being dug round Bandi Adhaim close to where the river emerges from the Jebel Hamrin. General Marshall marched on north and concentrated in front of this position by April 28th. Great heat and mirage impeded operations and reconnaissance. The aeroplane engines were worn out through continual flying without breathing space for overhaul, and failures had become so frequent as to impair the efficiency of the aerial arm. Since the beginning of operations in December the squadron had flown the equivalent of six full circuits of the world, no doubt a reason for many of the forced landings, the majority of the original machines being still in harness. To make matters worse, during the night of the 28/29th a terrific wind arose, and a dust-storm raged for two days, choking carburettors and bearings with sand, and almost tearing the aeroplanes away from the pegs and ropes with which they were tethered to the desert.

At 6 a.m. on the 28th Lieutenant Maguire went out on patrol but did not return. Captain Merton, who went in search, saw no trace, and he himself had a forced landing at Samarra. The German wireless told us that night that

Captain Schutz felled his eighth enemy aeroplane behind

our lines. The pilot was wounded and captured.

Poor Paddy, we never saw him again, for he died in a Turkish hospital at Tekrit. We missed him sadly.

On the 29th a Martinsyde on reconnaissance was blown upside down in the seventy mile an hour gale, and for ten minutes remained out of control. Three machines managed to co-operate with the artillery of Marshall's column and register the enemy positions before the attack. At dawn on the 30th there was a lull in the storm, when the Cheshires and South Wales Borderers advanced up the east bank of the Adhaim. The enemy position faced southerly astride the river-bed, and was refused back to the hills on either side.[3]

The intention was to drive in a wedge on his left flank and force him away from water and his line of retreat northeast. Demonstrations had been made against his right flank on the previous day. The Cheshires and Borderers charged across the fire-swept plain and gained all their objectives. Both battalions had started more than fifty *per cent*, under strength, and their casualties were heavy, including the colonel, adjutant, and nearly all the officers of the Cheshires. They saw "red," and swept beyond the village right on to the Turkish batteries. Four guns were captured, when down came the dust-storm and obliterated everything. The Turkish Commander saw his opportunity, and, masked by the storm, threw in an overwhelming counter-attack. The Cheshires and Borderers, isolated in the dust and a mile in front of their supports, were enveloped by the enemy, and died fighting hand-to-hand.

The enemy retook the village, but, being held up by the other two battalions of Lewin's brigade, never regained their lost trenches. The two front battalions had managed to send back one gun and 300 prisoners, including a brigadier, before they had been overwhelmed. Another attack, supported by intense artillery fire, regained us the village.

Under cover of the storm the enemy managed to strengthen

---

3. See sketch map.

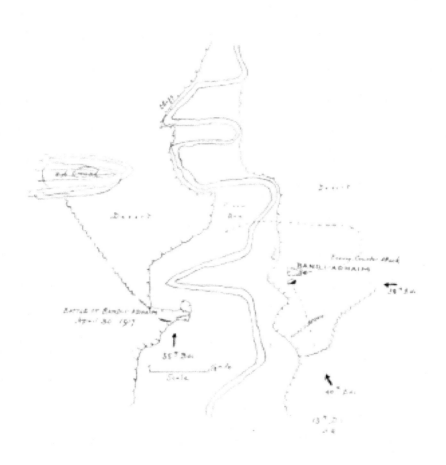

BATTLE OF BAND-I-ADHEIM

his left, which allowed him to make good his retreat after dark into the Jebel Hamrin. The battle had been bloody, and most of it bayonet work. Our casualties were severe, but we buried over 200 dead Turks and captured 365 prisoners, one gun, and much other booty.

One aeroplane had managed to co-operate early in the morning with the artillery bombardment, but the wild squalls and impenetrable dust driving as high as 5,000 feet made further aerial work impossible. Had it not been for the thundering gale and dust-screen the Turkish army would have experienced the greatest difficulty in making their escape.

On the morning of the 1st of May aerial reconnaissance located the enemy moving further back into the hills. It was decided to complete their discomfiture by an air raid on the 2nd. Six machines dropped half a ton of bombs on their columns, camps, and material, causing considerable damage and panic; at least fourteen bombs exploded in the centre of massed animals and men. News received three weeks later gave the enemy's casualties as fifty killed, including one regimental and one battalion commander, much damage to transport animals, and that a general officer, with his car, had been blown some yards off the road.

The enemy were now out of reach on all fronts, and Baghdad was for the present secure. The weather had become too hot for war, and casualties from heat impeded operations on the ground. The suffering of the troops in the desperate fighting of the last month had been severe; marching took place at night, but in the day rest on the hot ground under a burning sun was impossible. Often short of both water and rations, and with seldom any fresh food, the spirit throughout could only be regarded as superb. How it was recognised by the commander-in-chief is best understood in the following extract from his last despatch, dated 15th October, 1917, a few days before he himself was claimed by Mesopotamia:—

As a result of the fighting during April the enemy's 13th and 18th Corps had been driven back on divergent lines,

GENERAL MAUDE WITH BRITISH AND RUSSIAN STAFF OFFICERS

R.F.C. HEADQUARTER STAFF, BAGHDAD, SEPTEMBER 1917
CAPT. HUNTING CAPT. LILLEY CAPT. MOXEY
CAPT. NIXON LT.COL. MACEWAN LT.COL TENNANT MAJ. GRINLINGTON

the former into the Jebel Hamrin and the latter to Tekrit. The 13th Corps had twice taken the offensive, with results disastrous to itself, and the 18th Corps had been defeated and driven from its selected positions on four occasions. Our total captures for the month amounted to some 3,000 prisoners and seventeen guns, besides a considerable quantity of rolling-stock and booty of all kinds. The objectives which we had set out to enemy's troops was broken.

The fighting carried out during this month had imposed a severe strain upon the troops, for the heat, the constant dust-storms, and the absence of water on occasions, tested their stamina very highly. But as conditions became more trying the spirit of the troops seemed to rise, and at the end of this period they maintained the same high standard of discipline, gallantry in action, and endurance which had been so noticeable throughout the army during the operations which led to the fall of Baghdad and subsequently. The increasing heat now rendered it necessary that the troops should be redistributed for the hot weather, and that every provision possible under existing conditions should be made with a view to guarding against the trying period which was rapidly approaching. Whilst it was necessary to hold the positions which had been so bravely won, and to strengthen them defensively, the bulk of the troops were withdrawn into reserve and distributed in suitable camps along the river banks, where they could obtain the benefit of such breezes as were available, and where a liberal supply of water for drinking, bathing, and washing was obtainable.

On the Tigris line aerial reconnaissance reported the 18th Turkish Corps at Tekrit, and Cobbe's column occupied and made themselves secure at Samarra. The 13th Turkish Corps having retired on Kifri, General Marshall marched back down the Adhaim and took up a line of defence near its junction with the Tigris.

Of the two Flights at Barurah one was ordered back to Baghdad for overhaul of engines away from dust, and the other retired to Sindiyeh, forty miles north of Baghdad for counter aircraft duties and reconnaissance of the Tigris and Persian fronts. The remaining Flight remained at Baghdad for work on the Euphrates or as required. The British army sought shelter as best it could, for the oven door had closed on Mesopotamia.

CHAPTER 5

Days Grave and Gay

Up from Earth's Centre through the Seventh Gate
I rose, and on the Throne of Saturn sate,
And many Knots unravell'd by the Road;
But not the Knot of Human Death and Fate.
                                        —Omar.

The outposts counted the flies on their rifles; to the horizon there was no sign of a Turk. The ground forces had seen the last of the two enemy corps till the long summer should be over. But high overhead a low hum kept him ever aware of the vigilance of British eyes. It was now possible to send two or three machines in company on reconnaissance in case they should meet with a Halberstadt; flying on all fronts simultaneously was no longer required, and allowed concentration where necessary. Lieutenants Skinner and Lander attacked a Halberstadt over Tekrit on the 6th of May.

The enemy, taking full advantage of his climbing powers, was able to get on the tail of Lander's Martinsyde. The two machines, outstripping Skinner's B.E., were last seen still fighting and losing height three thousand feet above Tekrit. Enemy wireless reported later that Lander had been brought down by Sergeant-Major Pommerich, and was wounded and a prisoner. He had managed to land his machine on an island in the Tigris, and crawled out of it, one leg badly smashed by bullets. Arabs had swum across and stripped him of his clothing; then the Turks arrived and floated him to the mainland on a skin; just escaping drowning, he was dragged out, put on a horse, and arrived at Tekrit in serious condition.

Occasionally we heard of him: his broken bones would not heal; all that hot weather he lay eking out a miserable existence in the Turkish camps at Tekrit and Mosul. It was nine months before he could walk, but he survived, and turned up in Cairo a year and a half later. The German aviators were kind to him, and kept him supplied with any luxuries they had available.

Besides keeping a close watch on the enemy, the R.F.C. assisted at several punitive expeditions against hostile Arab tribes. Political officers were distributed throughout the occupied areas, but the Arab population were untrustworthy, and it was not safe to venture far from a British post without escort. They endeavoured to interfere with the Samarra railway, and wrecked a train in which the G.O.C. was travelling, fortunately in a rear truck. Lieutenant-Colonel Magniac was murdered while taking a walk near Felujah.

When such atrocities took place the Sheikh concerned would be ordered to deliver up the offenders for justice. After burning the villages, shooting some of the tribesmen, and confiscating their flocks, they generally came in and surrendered. On the Euphrates about Sumaikcheh, and up the Diala, no attention was paid to British authority, and it was necessary to send out small punitive expeditions. The heat made operations by day impossible; marching would be done by night and the villages surrounded and attacked at dawn.

The air unit was of extreme value in these circumstances, and eliminated the necessity of many such expeditions. If a tribe got out of hand a raid could leave the next morning and bomb and machine-gun any village within a 100-mile radius. Such immediate and drastic action inspired terror in the Arabs; once hunted down by machine-guns from the air they never wished a second dose, and a bomb having blotted out the happy home there was nought left but surrender.

With the cessation of fighting several of our observing officers left for Egypt or England to learn to fly. To fill their places a school .was started to train officers drafted from other units in the country, and to give selected artillery officers monthly courses in aerial co-operation. We had learnt much through experience, and a detailed system of instruction was instituted in order that we might be efficient and ready for any contingency when the weather got cool. A house on the right bank of the river was appropriated for this purpose and an elaborate mud model of the Istabulat position constructed in the courtyard.

The observer and his instructor controlled the fire from the roof, which was represented by the flashes of small electric lamps on the ground map. The effect was realistic, and gave a sound theoretical basis to work upon when taken into the air.

When we first arrived at Baghdad the R.F.C. occupied the railway workshops, but after the capture of Samarra the railway was reopened, and it was necessary to move to the wrecked German wireless house, which was used as an advanced aircraft park. The officers lived in houses on the right bank of the river. On the opposite bank P. S., the provost-marshal, and I had established ourselves in a house recently occupied by a Turkish officer. It was the usual square building with a courtyard in the middle opening through a heavy door into the street; within was a garden well-shaded by trees and palms, a fountain played in the centre, and a tiled path ran down to the balcony and landing-stage by the river.

Here, on a balmy night we would smoke an after-dinner *cheroot* under the big Eastern moon and watch the *mahalas* glide by. On arrival in March this garden was a mass of roses in bloom; it was impossible to resist the charm of the place. All houses in Baghdad had underground rooms, or *serdabs*, where the inhabitants retreated in the hot weather; we slept and dined on the roof, and these cellars in the daytime made life a luxury compared to the tents in the desert. We furnished this house from the bazaar, engaged a gardener and other native servants, and kept open house to our friends from the desert. The place was my home for a year, and I grew to be very fond of it.

D. H. organised one dinner-party of note at Baghdad; the

weather was hot, so guests were invited and a *gufa* (coracle) hired. In it were put table and chairs, and it was anchored off the shore and lit by electric light. The courses were rowed to and fro by chattering Arab servants. With the coffee and cigars the anchor was pulled up and we drifted downstream, to be eventually picked up and towed home by a motor-boat. It was a cheerful party, probably the first dinner-party that had ever taken place in an electrically-lit *gufa*.

Perhaps some had been looking forward to a period of ease after the weather became too hot to fight, but, at any rate among the organising departments, this was a misconception. All intelligence seemed to point to a great effort by the Central Powers. We in Mesopotamia had at least to prepare resistance against a bold bid for Baghdad by the Turks in the coming cool season. Russia had crumbled, thereby exposing our right flank to new dangers from the Caspian. Agents brought news of the advance of the Baghdad railway towards Nisibin and the improvement of the Euphrates road for motor transport. We heard tell of newly-numbered German Divisions dressed for a hot climate; of train-loads of guns, ammunition, and lorries rumbling eastwards from Stamboul. Was their destination Palestine or Mesopotamia, or both?

The wires were busy between Baghdad, Cairo, and London, and the Intelligence sweated far into the night. In response to many appeals an additional squadron could at last be spared for Mesopotamia, and General Maude accepted the offer of two R.F.C. Kite Balloon Sections. The R.N.A.S. Kite Balloon Section had packed up after the advance on Baghdad, and their personnel left for other scenes of action. Kite Balloons seemed to me of no use in mobile warfare, and certainly could not operate in the hot weather. They were an expensive item, and involved much extra transport.

However, they were already starting for the East when I first heard of the proposal. There was only a short time in which to prepare for this trebled strength. It meant a large expansion in the Aircraft Park; detailed calculations of estimates for stores six months ahead (there were more than a thousand different store items); the construction of hangars at Samarra and Baghdad, for which every piece of wood and canvas had to be imported into the country; provision of extra barges and steamers on the river, and a million other requirements. All this when labour and material were being taxed to their utmost in the building of railways, bridges, bunds, hospital huts, and other military necessities.

We formed a Wing Headquarters out of the officers and clerks available, rolled up our sleeves, and did a bit of thinking. It would have been too easy in Europe, but it was different a few thousand miles from nowhere. India was requisitioned for a solid form of hangar for the Aircraft Park; they were delayed for want of girders which had to come from England. Those hangars arrived more than a year later, after I had gone and the war was almost over.

Meanwhile the great work in hand was mapping. We must have accurate, detailed maps of the country on all fronts and beyond, ready for autumn eventualities. Photography grew to a scale that exceeded the stock of plates for which we had estimated; India collected from Calcutta to Bombay, and relieved the situation pending the arrival of hundreds of dozens from England. They deteriorated rapidly in the climate, and special refrigerating plant had to be imported to cool the water for developing and printing. (This also proved useful in cooling our drinks.) The office worked at high pressure and the temperature was higher; fans had been imported and made a hot gale over one's head; the wind outside covered the papers with a coating of dust and then the fans scattered them over the floor. One sat all day and half the night while the sweat dropped on to the foolscap until the ink ran.

Hangars gradually came up river, but meanwhile the old B.E.s and Martinsydes shrivelled in the sun and their engines choked with desert sand. Their fabric became bleached and loose, one could poke one's finger through it; to have looped one of these machines would have been courting disaster. A machine in Egypt had collapsed in the air owing to the dryness of the wood. The demise of this pilot was a warning to us, and the veterans which had been long in the sun were handled cautiously.

In the middle of May I flew down river to Aircraft Park. A chain of landing grounds was selected at the British posts of Bghailah, Sheikh Saad, and Amara, where mechanics were established. It was a protracted journey, against contrary winds, but interesting to see all the old haunts and battlefields again. The army that once had populated and civilised such places as Arab Village, Sinn and Sheikh Saad had passed on.

There was nothing left to indicate to a newcomer that what now was desert had once been a city of tents and war stores, scenes of activity and thick population. The country had gone back to its state of desolation. Amara had become a still larger hospital city; the tents extended further into the desert. It was also a busy centre of the Inland Water Transport. There was a remount depot, convalescent camp, and rest camp for passing soldiers.

A metre-gauge railway linked it with Kurnah to relieve some of the shipping in this section, where the river is so narrow that only one ship can go through at a time. Three or four spare aeroplanes were housed at Amara ready to reinforce the Front, and the R.F.C. maintained a rest camp, accommodation, and messing arrangements for passing pilots. Our camp was pleasantly situated in a date grove, and weary pilots and observers given a few days' leave from the front were glad to get there for a few days' respite from war. There were tennis courts, a club, and the society of the fair sex from the hospitals, to brighten the eye and fan the embers of forgotten civilisation. It was a cheerful place, Amara.

Down at Busrah the air was damp and the mosquitoes troublesome, but it was good to be at a harbour again; to hear the ocean-going steamers passing in the river, and lie awake at night and listen to the hoots of their syrens. There is something romantic about a harbour, any harbour. In my old age give me a harbour with the sounds of ships, the curious foreign sailor-folk, God's fresh air, and the tang of the sea.

In the evenings at Busrah, Clarke, of the Aircraft Park, and myself would go out in a motorboat and board British-India steamers trooping between Bombay and the Gulf. The white paint and spotless decks of a passenger liner were a relief to the eye after life ashore, the hospitality of their officers was unlimited, and many a pleasant evening we spent in that breathless tideway, smoking in deck chairs under the bridge, exchanging experiences of sea, land, and air.

The lot of these seamen during the war was a laborious one. After a few summers in the Gulf they would have changed gladly for some more invigorating sphere and a chance of blotting a "Fritz." Short of staff, ever on the move, and perpetually in the wet steam of the Gulf, there was no rest year in year out. They did their bit. In earlier days to get a square meal at Busrah, unless an officer belonged to one of the permanent base establishments, he had to repair on board a steamer and beg a place in the saloon. The B.I. captains saved many an army subaltern from going hungry.

The river craft, originally manned and administered by the Royal Indian Marine, had now come under the control of the Inland Water Transport (Royal Engineers), so the sailor-men changed their white drill for khaki, and became soldiers *pro tem*. The skipper of a tug disguised himself as a sergeant-major R.E., and the captains of the larger vessels as subalterns or captains in the army. Of these seamen who had volunteered for the Tigris some came from river-boats on the Yukon, some from the Irrawaddy or Brahmaputra, others from blue water. It seemed incongruous to meet the ex-captain of an 8,000-ton tramp navigating a shallow-draught paddle-boat in the uniform of a second lieutenant R.E.

The flight up to Baghdad was slow; coming down there had been a buffeting south wind; on the journey north the wind had changed there, too. After a few flights between the base and front they became intensely boring, but the mode of progression saved many days, and even weeks, when the river was low. An aeroplane from Busrah was always well loaded with the R.F.C.

mail and important official letters; there were also purchases executed for the mess to be taken back; these cargoes varied from polo sticks to bottles of champagne. The Indian merchants and Expeditionary Force Canteen did big business at Busrah.

How well I remember those flights; the preparation of the machine before the sun rose, the difficulties of stowage for what appeared an impossible load, the roll of bedding eventually lashed on to the centre section struts; the sticky run across the soft salt soil of the Busrah aerodrome, and the small margin of clearance over the sheds; a wave to the cheery park commander and his men on the ground; a last look at the harbour, and then, steadying on to the course, one settled down into one's seat and hummed and droned, droned and hummed, ever northward. In case of a forced landing the rule was to follow the river, but, with the gliding distance of 6,000 feet and confidence in a good engine, many miles could be cut off by a more direct course across its wide deviations.

The long straight reach to Kurnah had the appearance of a colourless canal bordered by a thin strip of date-palms. The country below was flat sandy desert. Far ahead, but sharply defined through the haze, the desert ended against a dark blur. One came to this in time, the beginning of the swamps; they stretched to the horizon on either hand, a mass of bleak vegetation growing out of sapphire pools. It was most noticeable, this colour of the marsh water, as compared with that of the Tigris, and where it drained into the river the blue showed in contrast to the mud-coloured stream.

Yet it was only Tigris water going back to Tigris; a hundred miles ahead, at Amara, the river bifurcates east into the canal, which distributes itself over a vast tract of country into small canals and wide swamps. Here and there were dry patches of cleared ground thickly populated by Marsh Arabs, a low and undeveloped type of humanity unknown to the white man except near the main channels. Their country is impenetrable. The Tigris between Kurnah and Amara is narrow and tortuous, and it is difficult for the pilot to discern the main stream out of the various channels among the swamps below. Only the shipping gave the clue to the newcomer, the craft here and there looking like stationary specks, the white wash churned by their paddles like the stream from a mill.

There was nowhere to land in the event of engine-failure over these swamps. With the day growing hot, one was glad to go down at Amara, yell for Bob, the Madrassi cook, to bring breakfast, and then lie and sweat in the tent till the sun got low. With the slow old B.E.s one had the choice of going on against the prevailing north wind to Sheikh Saad the same evening or staying the night comfortably at Amara and pushing through to Baghdad the following morning.

The latter was the cooler plan. Off before the dawn, not too low over the hospital at the risk of a letter from the medical authorities concerning the shattered nerves of sick colonels, and one struck north again with the river on the left. It was a wearisome desert flight to Sheikh Saad; a north-westerly cut led you across the Tigris and left Ali Gharbi far to the north, where the river turns west; the Pusht-i-Kuh stood out like a wall just beyond.

One crossed a remote flooded area and eventually met the river again at Sheikh Saad. Here, the previous year, the authorities had planned to irrigate a few acres for the cultivation of vegetables. There was still a post at Sheikh Saad, and the "market garden" was in being. It was the cause of a remarkable and awkward phenomenon on this occasion. I intended to land, and came low over the cultivated patch; above it was a zone of turbulation, gusty currents of air seemed to come from every direction, the machine would first bump up 200 feet, then drop 400 feet like a stone; she was utterly out of control until I glided well past into the desert again.

As the aerodrome lay adjacent to the cultivation it would have been inadvisable to attempt a landing, and I perforce had to miss my breakfast and continue on to Bghailah, over old battlefields the whole way. From Bghailah to Baghdad one was seldom far from the river; at 9,000 feet over Azizieh the sum-

140

mits of the Persian hills loomed above the haze, many leagues to starboard, and the Diala glinted like a steel ribbon across one's path. The dark shade beyond suggested Baghdad.

On May 13th it was evident that the enemy had imported, in addition to their single-seater fighting machines, a new and faster type of two-seater Albatross. Merton, in a Bristol Scout, encountered one of these over Deli Abbas. The combat began by a steep dive by the Bristol, which dislodged the pilot's sun-helmet, considerably baulking his aim and fire. A passenger made his appearance from inside the fuselage of the Hun and opened fire with a rear machine-gun. The Bristol's gun was hit and damaged, causing the explosion of two cartridges. Merton had judged the machine a single-seater, and fit to be attacked from behind, so that the appearance of an observer came as a surprise. Being *hors-de-combat*, Merton broke off the encounter, and returned unpursued to his aerodrome. It had been a close call for M.

Our anti-aircraft gunners received encouragement about this time in the following copy of a Turkish message which fell into our hands:

The German aviator told me that he could not report clearly on the body of troops north of Samarra this morning, as the fire of the British Anti-Aircraft was very heavy and accurate.

One can imagine the reception afforded to the British pilot who would volunteer such a report!

As the days grew hotter enemy aerial activity became negligible, and by the end of May already seven of our own pilots had gone to hospital.

The Turkish forces remained out of touch to the north-east about Kifri, on the Tigris at Tekrit, and on the Euphrates at Ramadi. Leave to India had been opened for those officers and men of the force who could be spared, but with numbers thinned down by sickness, the necessity for permanent activity, and only No. 30 Squadron to cover all fronts, few could be released for a spell in the cool of the Himalayas, for three weeks in India entailed an absence of two months by the time the journeys to and from the front were taken into account.

Nevertheless, many of Force "D" managed to migrate to Gulmarg, in Kashmir, or Neuralia, in Ceylon, and returned with talk of cool mountain air, ecstatic scenery, grass and green things; wine, women, and song. It all sounded idyllic to us jaded and dried-up folk who had remained behind.

The night of the 4th of June was celebrated over the Turkish lines. Dent, of the Intelligence, came with me, and we reconnoitred the enemy positions and camps up the Tigris by the light of a full desert moon. It was a wonderful night, milky blue and beautiful. We started from Baghdad, dined and fuelled with the Flight at Sindiyeh, and went on north. Observations were as easy as by daylight, and flying much more pleasant; the silver trail of the Tigris took us there and back.

The enemy picked us up at 4,000 feet and shelled wildly; being shelled in the air by night is, I think, even worse than by day; the blinding flashes of the bursts, above, underneath, and around, add a dazzling and eerie effect to the usual crashing chaos of an air barrage. Dent was taking notes rapidly while I dropped parachute flares to light up the shadows below. His work finished, he turned round and waved a hand, and, to rout them all out, we dived to 1800 feet and machine-gunned the camp. Both guns splayed bullets till our ammunition was gone, and we left the place to clear up its confusion and vanished south into the night, followed by the crackling of rifles and machine-guns.

At 1 a.m. we refuelled at Sindiyeh and flew on to Baghdad. The outline of mosques and minarets against the sapphire of the twinkling sky, the moonlight thrown back off the blue-tiled domes, and the great stillness over all; was it a dream or could it be real? The following night Captains Bayly and O'Neill did the same reconnaissance as a check. In each case the flight lasted five hours from Baghdad.

The river had started to fall, and in order to keep the Flight up the Tigris supplied by river transport, and to prevent the workshop and store barge from being marooned until the autumn, it was necessary to drop sixteen miles downstream into deeper water at Sadeah, on the left bank. In the high-water a fly-boat had managed to navigate beyond Samarra, but the larger boats could not penetrate above Barurah. The Tigris winds over mud and sand to the sea, with a drop of only a few feet in its six-hundred mile journey; but above here the whole aspect of the river changes; its bed becomes rocky, there are numerous islands, and it flows swiftly between cliffs with sections of cataract, like the Nile above Haifa.

The weather became hotter, although the *shamal* had started earlier than usual. The noonday shade temperature in June was generally 112 deg. Fahr., and by four in the afternoon we "ink-slingers" in Baghdad became wound up and short of temper. Man changes under these conditions for the worse; hard work and loss of health alter perspective, and are a tax that tells even on the sunniest characters. A few months of it and life seems to fade yellow, only when the sun has at last dropped "below the yard-arm," and one may get outside several whiskies-and-sodas does one's outlook revive. You must work through a hot weather in the East before you are qualified to criticise the actions of your less fortunate fellows:

The temper of chums, the love of a wife, or a new piano's tune, which of the three will you trust at the end of an Indian June?

Kipling struck the note true.

Polo saved our lives those stifling months. The G.O.C. Re-mounts and his staff of sportsmen overcame the pony difficulty; many of the Indian polo ponies were in Mesopotamia; we were well mounted and the game was as keen as the heat would allow.

We played for forty-five minutes before sundown; riding out to the desert ground the walls of the houses threw off their heat enough to blister your face, you could not leave your hand on them. The ground itself was red-hot, and pony and rider played in a welter of sweat which filled one's boots, but the sun was down, the glare had gone, and the physical exertion was good. In the days at Arab Village we had played almost within sight of the Turk whenever there was a chance; the polo in Mesopotamia was the big asset compared with the war in other theatres.

In June the Russians announced that they could endure the heat on the Diala no longer, and fell back to the mountain regions about Karind and Kirmanshah, leaving our right flank exposed. Beled Ruz was therefore occupied by the cavalry.

The army had settled down to hide from the sun as best it might. The cavalry division were encamped in a date grove on the river three miles north of Baghdad. The 3rd Corps dug themselves under the desert, the 13th Division about Sindiyeh, on the left bank of the Tigris; and the 14th about Baqubah, on the Diala. The 1st Corps had taken up a strong defensive position at Samarra, and the 15th Division, who had come up from Nasiriyeh, were at Felujah. Enemy aircraft were occasionally reported.

Their usual formation appeared to be one or two Albatrosses in company with a Halberstadt escorting at higher altitude. Air patrols were out in the early mornings, but he was seldom encountered. His aerodromes were at Kifri and Tekrit. He bombed our camps at Samarra, Beled, and Baqubah once in June; no casualties were inflicted, as most of his bombs were "duds." In reply, six B.E.s retaliated on the camps at Tekrit; seven tents were demolished by direct hits.

On the 22nd June Captain Bayly and Lieutenant Skinner attacked an enemy ship aground ten miles north of Tekrit; one bomb exploded in the after-part and another blew in her side.

Training for the coming winter campaign went on in the early hours. A regular series of practice shots at desert targets with the artillery took place; the Akkarkuf Lake, outside Baghdad, afforded a good range for aerial gunnery, over which machines would manoeuvre, shooting at each other's shadows on the water.

On the evening of 25th June, while having dinner on my roof, a messenger arrived with a note from General Maude, asking if it was feasible that he should fly to Samarra and back on the following afternoon in order to give away a cup to the winning team of the 7th Division football competition. It was a night's journey to Samarra by rail, and unless he flew it meant being away two nights and a day from G.H.Q., which he could ill afford. I did not like the idea of trusting one's engine in the heat of the afternoon and the possibility of a forced landing "in the blue" with the commander-in-chief—he had never flown before—but the plan seemed so sporting that I decided to rely on Fortune, and wrote him that it could be done.

We kept quiet about it, and not even G.H.Q. knew until the expectant G.O.C. 7th Division telegraphed asking how General Maude intended arriving, as he had not come by the night train. I arranged for an escort machine in case of trouble, and before starting asked the C.-in-C. what he desired me to do if we met a Hun. We were only in an old B.E., in which the result of a scrap depended on the efficiency of the observer with the gun. It was inadvisable for the general to work the observer's gun; he was too big to move in the cramped seat, and would probably only have shot away the wires or propeller. His reply was "Shoot him down," so, with the pilot's gun only, I set off, fervently praying that the evening was too hot for any Hun to come up.

The strong *shamal* delayed us, but we arrived at Samarra, without incident, in time to witness the second half of the match. The cup was duly presented to the winners, the Black Watch, and, with the sun setting, we started our hundred mile run back to Baghdad. There was only a quarter moon, and I knew we should have to land in the dark, but the G.O.C. seemed to have no qualms whatever, and gaily started off; if he had known more about flying perhaps he would have stayed the night; for me *twas folly to be wise*. I wired for flares to be put out; the machine went perfectly, and only bumped slightly on landing, at 8.45 p.m. in the dark. General Maude had enjoyed himself, the story went round, and the army was vastly pleased.

At dawn on July 3rd a punitive column arrived about Beled Ruz to deal with the Beni Tamin tribe, who had been actively hostile since our arrival at Baghdad. Two aeroplanes co-operated with bombs and Lewis guns. They discovered the tribesmen in mass awaiting the advance of our troops. As a preliminary two 65 lb. bombs burst where they were thickest, causing confusion and dismay; six more bombs fell among them, and they scattered in all directions. Further bombs set their village on fire. That was the end. To quote the official report:

> Artillery and the unexpected aerial attack which got home into Beni Tamin, who were apparently preparing to get mounted to oppose our troops, demoralised them.

It did.

General Maude now determined to improve our position on the Euphrates and occupy Zibban, the junction of the Saklaw-ieh Canal, by which Lake Akkarkuf was flooded, and to consolidate this occupation by surprising Ramadi. The capture of the latter place would also complete our blockade of the Turk from the rich Euphrates country, whence Arabs were supplying him, *via* a caravan route from Kerbela. The weather had been growing daily hotter; the Turks would deem any operation at this time of year impossible, and were no doubt absorbed with their own condition, hundreds of miles from any base, and envying us the shade around Baghdad.

Perhaps there was a chance that such a *coup* might succeed, but it seemed impossible that troops could march, let alone fight, in that flaming temperature. They moved forward from Felujah by night, and occupied Zibban on the morning of July 8th. The enemy must have had wind of the movement, unless it was mere chance that brought two Hun aeroplanes over our troops on the Diala on the 7th; air patrols sent to cut them off on the Tigris never found them, and the next report was that they were seen going west over Felujah. It was presumed that they had descended at Ramadi, and would return to their base either at Tekrit or Kifri in the cool of the next morning.

A patrol was sent out to waylay them on the morning of the 8th, but the hostile machines were not seen. On the evening of the 9th it was reported that they had left Ramadi that morning, and "Intelligence" reported that one of them had come down in the desert. The weather was frantic; a regular heat wave consumed the country. By 11 a.m. on the 9th the thermometer stood at 122 deg. Fahr. in the shade. A strong wind had sprung up which dried the moisture out of the eyes until they became so bloodshot it was difficult to see. I lunched with Buxton, of the *Mantis*, under double awnings and behind a screen on deck. Baghdad was enveloped in a haze of sand and a scorching gale. The glasses we drank out of were too hot to hold, and had to be cooled with the ration of ice, which the Supply and Transport Corps now manufactured in the town. The plates, knives, and forks, everything was burning.

Men were dropping like flies with heatstroke; the hospitals could take no more, they were lying in rows between the beds. There is no time to waste in heatstroke; a man fit and well will be suddenly seized, and if he is not better is dead in two or three hours. The supply of ice was limited; many of those lying recovering from disease were seized as they lay. The nurses worked night and day through it all without respite; they were magnificent. Worn out and ill themselves, they fought desperately in the breathless wards for the lives of the men. Those nights sleep was impossible; on the roof of my house it was necessary to pour water continually over the sheet I was lying on to prevent it scorching one's body; a little longer and there would not be much left of the British Force in Mesopotamia.

One wondered what on earth was happening on the Euphrates. On the 10th General Andrews concentrated a column at Zibban, and was ready to move forward on Ramadi. He had an unenviable task. The plan was to make a surprise attack at dawn against the enemy's northern flank, and endeavour to get between him and the Euphrates. Cavalry and armoured cars were to await developments on the extreme right under cover of date-groves on the river bank, and four machines were detached to Felujah to work with the column.

Arrangements were made to keep the troops supplied with

ice and drinking water by Ford vans. In the dawn I motored across the forty miles of desert to Felujah to arrange for the air co-operation on the following day. I and my driver started back in the heat of the day without waiting till evening. As long as I live I shall never forget that drive. There was no canopy over the Hupmobile car, any part of which was almost too hot to touch. The "weight" of the sun on one's head made one stupid, and by the time we reached the edge of Lake Akkarkuf there was no water left with which to refill the radiator, again almost empty.

It was a narrow shave; if we had had to walk I do not think we could have gone very far. We soaked our spine-pads and clothing in the water, cooled our helmets, and refilled the radiator. Entering the semi-dark arched bazaars of Baghdad was entering Heaven after the Fury outside. It felt like an ice-house, though in reality over 120 deg. Fahr.; the Baghdadis themselves had no record of such heat for scores of years. That drive put us both on our backs till the next day.

It was of no use for General Andrews to wait till the Turks improved their defences; he must either go on in the heat or go back. His column moved forward that, night of the 10th, which was hotter even than before. As many men as possible were carried in lorries and Ford vans. They deployed at 4 a.m. on the 11th, and drove in the enemy out-posts. By 8 a.m. the heat and a scorching dust- storm were opponents of greater moment than the enemy.

Observation was impossible, the men were dropping wholesale with heatstroke, almost all the officers of the Dorset Regiment had succumbed, the sun was getting worse every minute, and the Turkish shell-fire more accurate. The attack had to be discontinued, and the men lay down for the day to endure as best they might. Aerial co-operation was maintained till 10 a.m. Two Martinsydes and a B.E. had left Baghdad at 4.30 a.m. to bomb and machine-gun and generally harass the enemy, but the two Martinsydes were forced down again even at that hour; their water boiled away and the pilots sick with the heat. Lieutenant Rose got away in the B.E. and blew up a Turkish ammunition wagon with a direct hit.

Captain V. Buxton, from my H.Q., had accompanied a wireless ground station. It was spotted on the open plain by the Turkish gunners, and came under heavy and accurate shell-fire. The aerial was shot away three times, but Buxton and the operator Hall re-erected it each time, and, still under heavy fire, eventually succeeded in establishing communication with the aeroplane, thus enabling two enemy guns to be silenced. At night it was possible for the exhausted troops to retire to the river bank, where they found shade for the next day. On the 14th they withdrew to Zibban, pressed by 1,500 Arab tribesmen. The operations had been a failure, but there are limits to the power of humanity, and strings of motor-ambulances winding back to Baghdad told the tale of the weather more than the accuracy of the Turkish gunners.

No more had been heard of the two enemy aeroplanes; in an effort to locate these tortured antagonists in case they were stranded in that weather, a patrol of our machines searched the desert on the morning of the 10th without result. But two German aviators—an officer and an N.C.O.—staggered into Samarra in an exhausted and gave themselves up to a picquet of the 7th Division. Their story was grim. They confirmed that they had left Ramadi for Tekrit on the morning of the 9th, when one of the pair of Albatrosses was forced to land due to the engine seizing up in the intense heat.

The second machine also landed, and after burning the first, they started off again, four up, with one on each wing. Besides the four men the aeroplane carried its own machine-guns plus one salved off No. 1, all the personal kit belonging to the men, four carbines, 900 rounds of ammunition, and a small Persian dog which habitually accompanied reconnaissances as a mascot. With this load they flew for twenty-five minutes at an altitude of 400 feet, but the height was insufficient to keep the engine cool, and a descent became necessary.

The aviators therefore decided to wait in the desert till evening, and sheltered underneath the wings of the aeroplane.

The temperature was beyond 122 deg. Fahr. in the shade, and they can have only had unsatisfactory shade from their machine; there was a strong wind blowing whose temperature was higher. After some hours, tortured by thirst, they drank the almost boiling water out of the radiator. At 6.30 p.m. they again started, hoping to reach the Tigris by "taxying," but the engine soon seized up, and they were obliged to burn machine No. 2, and endeavour to reach the river on foot. They marched till 8 p.m., when an officer and N.C.O. collapsed.

The other two, Captain von Gröne, and a sergeant-major, reached our picquet line completely exhausted at 5.30 a.m. the morning of the 10th. The G.O.C. 1st Corps sent out armoured cars and cavalry with one of the Germans as guide, but they failed to find either machines or men, although the search went out on two mornings. They must have died very soon of exhaustion and thirst. The thought of it made the strife of mankind seem puny.

Von Gröne came down to Baghdad. He was a Death's Head Hussar, and had only been East a month. There was nothing Hunnish apparent in von Gröne. The Intelligence Department got little from him, and his manners and reticence, in spite of the terrible ordeal he had just come through and the fact that he was ill, could only arouse respect. He gave us news of Lander, who had been shot down on May 6th with a damaged engine, and was now in hospital at Tekrit with six bullet wounds in the leg. We also learnt that poor Paddy Maguire had come down in flames, and died of his burns ten days later.

The heat wave did not abate, but the midday shade temperature rose to 123 deg. Fahr.; inside tents it was 136 deg. Fahr. The sickness rose, too. D. H. went down with heatstroke, but was pulled through. The Chief of the Staff, Sir Arthur Money, just returned from leave, also went down, but lived to be invalided out of the country.

Two of our mechanics died on consecutive days; one officer and six other mechanics were invalided the same week; seven officers and thirty-two men of the squadron were in hospital;

and out of the seven new pilots arrived to reinforce the thinned numbers of No. 30 Squadron three went into hospital at Busrah and one was put ashore from the river-boat on reaching Kut. Far from building up our strength for the autumn campaigning we were ebbing away to nothing. For a few days there was only one officer fit to fly, so I augmented the strength of the squadron by taking on the duties of flying officer in the mornings myself. It was not often in the war that numbers were so reduced that the wing commander had to act also as flying officer, but we had to carry on.

On the 15th July I decided to go down river to Busrah to make final preparations for the arrival of No. 63 Squadron, now somewhere between the Cape of Good Hope and the Persian Gulf. "Tiger Lily," the wing equipment officer, was to have accompanied me, but the heat was too much for him, having already been invalided out of the country in earlier days; he had never really recovered, yet carried on in a wonderful fashion, although only fit to crawl between his office and his bed. "Edgar R.," the photographic officer, came instead, and we made a curious passage to Busrah in the old *Bahmanshir* at the very height of the heat.

That appalling journey downstream has ever since been a firm bond of union between "Edgar R." and myself. We had the ship to ourselves, and took a servant to cook our food. The awning on deck was only of single thickness, and during the day it was necessary to lie in the deck- cabin; even inside the cabin the rays seemed to penetrate the deck, for at high noon one had to wear a helmet to avoid a headache.

A year later, at Lahore, in the Punjab, I was reminded of this by having to do the same thing sitting at *tiffin* inside a bungalow; a modern one—the old-fashioned ones were built thicker. The whole journey down we wore nought else but a bath-towel round our waists and spent the day in hoisting buckets of water from the warm Tigris and pouring it over our bodies; the immediate evaporation in the hot wind made a delicious chill for about thirty seconds, till it dried off again, the wind scorched, and the proceeding had to be repeated. It sounds ludicrous now, but I think it kept us both from going down with heatstroke. I remember we could not walk on the deck with bare feet under the awning, but had to wear shoes to prevent being scorched.

"Edgar R." and I kept quite fit in spite of the awful weather; we ate little, but lived on stout, another tip to the uninitiated. It was a record low river, and we often stuck on the ground; but the old *Bahmanshir*, with her courteous old Arab skipper, vibrated into Busrah five days later. Although the heat had been its fiercest, I think we were both refreshed by a rest from the work and worries of the last three months; we slept a little, laughed a little, drank a good deal, and sweated a lot. There was work on hand at Busrah, but the air hung dank and heavy; the humidity made it far worse than upriver. A wet 110 deg. Fahr. is ten times more trying than a dry 130 deg. Fahr.

Everyone at the base seemed more dead than alive, and it was impossible to get anything done. There was little use going to bed at nights; we would search the harbour in a motor-boat for a region of cooler air without success; everything was damp, for the wind blew off the Gulf. After a few fitful moments of sleep between midnight and 4 a.m. one would wake up feeling like a wet rag, and perhaps take a motor-bicycle out into the desert, away from the river, in quest of a cool breath.

There was none. By eight the thermometer was back over the 100, and at breakfast the same wag would daily play "The End of a Perfect Day" on the gramophone. We were issued with large Japanese parasols to keep our helmets cool. A British officer presented a comic sight in shirt-sleeves, shorts, blue goggles, a large helmet, a spine pad, and over all a huge parasol! It was with looks of longing that one watched the great white hospital ships gliding down the harbour with their cargoes of wrecked humanity bidding farewell to this benighted country for ever.

Nevertheless Busrah was always cheerful, for one ran up against many friends at the base. I found my friend "Bottle," of the 14th, just back from leave in Kashmir, endeavouring to drown dull care in lime juice at the Club in the heat of the day; then there was Cartwright, of the *Moth*, just up from doing guardship at Fao, he and all his crew nearly silly with prickly-heat. We all had it at Busrah; it spoils life entirely. According to Cartwright, Busrah was a health resort compared with Fao.

I flew down across the Karun River with Clarke to the Anglo-Persian Oil Company at Abadan. We had been endeavouring for some time to use their petrol in our aero-engines, but, in spite of distilling a lighter spirit than was shipped from Egypt or Burma, and eliminating its sulphuric properties, all attempts to use it had failed. Engines ran hot and seized up. Its use would have involved great saving in shipping and worries as to timely arrivals of supplies, which sometimes, when ships were overdue, ran down to a very low ebb, and on occasions had only been rushed upriver in time to save the situation.

We were importing 10,000 gallons a month solely for flying purposes. The motor-transport of the army ran entirely on this Anglo-Persian spirit, and the wells were invaluable in supplying oil fuel for the river craft and locomotives, which had been adapted to its use, thus saving the importation of coal. It was interesting to be shown over these famous refineries, the original cause of the despatch of an expeditionary force from India. Here a handful of Scotsmen and an army of Persians and local Arabs refined and directed the flow of oil from the 100-mile pipe-line to supply Jellicoe in the North Sea.

The settlement consisted of rows of huge tanks and a smattering of houses made of red brick, with wide verandas; it had its own hospital. The heat was appalling; the company's officials were there through the war without a break, a trying life for white man or black. We lunched with the manager and his wife, and then flew back to Busrah. After a week at the base I was glad to get away up-country again to the drier atmosphere of the desert. But a fortnight later I once more left Baghdad, this time by air to meet No. 63 Squadron on its arrival from England.

I had just cleared the Baghdad aerodrome on the morning of the 11th August, when, at a low height, my engine cut out; there was no room to turn and glide back, and nothing for it but to descend straight into a quarry. I took it as slow as possible, about forty-eight miles an hour; nevertheless, the crash was complete. Fortunately there was no one in the front seat, or he would have been killed. As it was I only cut my chin and knee, and a few stitches in both places by a doctor roused from slumber at a neighbouring field ambulance put me right.

It was urgent that I should get to Busrah, so a start was made in another machine. A favourable wind blew me to Amara in one reach, but my knee had swollen up, and I had to be helped out of the machine. Lying up in the tent all day did not improve matters, and, not being able to walk, there was nothing for it but to go to hospital. Lieutenant Morris, who had accompanied me in another machine, flew on with all the necessary papers and instructions for the new squadron, and I arrived a week later. The weather at Busrah had not improved.

No. 63 Squadron had arrived on the 13th August. I suppose eighty *per cent*, of their officers were under twenty-four years of age, some under twenty, and the age of the other ranks must have been similar. It was a hard test for a youngster to arrive straight from England into such a climate. Till they arrived in port the health of the squadron had been excellent, but the Busrah climate immediately drove fifty *per cent*, into hospital; two died of heatstroke within the first few days.

They were a well-trained crowd, mostly air veterans from the Western Front, and they arrived with a morale superb, ready to finish the war. But climate had been out of their reckoning, and by the time I arrived the remaining half had mostly succumbed. Of thirty officers only six remained, and of two hundred odd men only seventy. This remnant was lying on its back at Aircraft Park, and even those who could stand up ware badly shaken. I had feared such a debacle. Busrah was doing its "damndest" to destroy humanity.

At the Aircraft Park there were about sufficient left to make up the funeral parties in the evening. I spent the whole of one afternoon rubbing C., a new pilot, with ice from the chest that kept the soda-water cool. He had rolled over with heatstroke while taking an afternoon *siesta*. We pulled him round just before the last small lump of ice melted away. Disease shakes the morale of men a thousand times more acutely than the worst shell-fire. There was practically no evaporation in the air, and it is by evaporation that humans retain their normal temperature. The doctors were unwilling to speculate what would happen if the wet bulb went up another degree.

I had a parade the first evening; it was all they could do to come out and stand at attention the while I recounted beautiful lies about the bracing climate, and forbade anybody else to get ill. The next day the worst happened, for I was laid prone myself with a violent attack of fever and carried off with the others to a congested hospital! The disembarkation of aeroplanes, transport, and stores was entirely held up, for there was no one to work. One could only wait anxiously for a moderation of the heat.

Meanwhile we lay with flaming temperature in the packed wards, and further cargoes of sick arriving from upriver made the congestion worse. Part of the nurses' quarters were utilised as hospitals, and the hospital ships filled for India as soon as possible to make room for others. Delirious men rambled on through the long hot nights, and one only thought of when the angel nurse would return down the row of beds with fresh ice to chill the towel round one's head. I had become well acquainted with fever and Mesopotamian hospitals, but some of these boys fresh from their English homes were hard hit. In time we went down to the convalescent hospital at Beit Naama to regain some weight; the terrible weather that had prevailed for a month had gone, and the air was dry, the temperature back to its normal at 115 deg. Fahr. at noon.

I returned to the Aircraft Park, where yet little sign of life was showing. Clarke was a marvel; he seemed to thrive in Busrah, and his spirits never left their zenith, in spite of having been there for two years without leave. There was no sign of 63 Squadron; with dismay I read the medical reports of some being invalided out of the country and others seriously ill; malaria, dysentery, sand-fly fever and heatstroke had taken heavy toll. There was big work to be done in the coming winter, and the Huns were reinforced with new aeroplanes; 30 Squadron was thinned out by sickness and short of machines, yet the base was crowded with unpacked cases of aeroplanes and engines. The personnel had melted away; we waited anxiously for them to emerge from the hospitals. One felt that anyway the situation could get no worse, and things must begin to take shape again soon.

The R.E. 8 type of aeroplane had arrived in quantity for both squadrons; also the long-awaited fighting scouts known as Spads. There was no lack of material, including the rows of Crossley light lorries for desert transport. But every engine had to be taken down and overhauled; the aeroplane wooden parts had shrunk in the heat, necessitating the rebuilding of many machines.

The task of the Park was immense. We got the first Spad put together and I took her up; she very nearly caused The End; the cooling arrangements devised for Europe were inadequate, and the water started boiling as I left the ground. I shoved her up to try and get into cooler atmosphere. At 6,000 feet over the harbour I was suddenly aware of the whole top plane warping into wave-like contortions and steam scalding my face. The auxiliary water-tank in the plane had exploded and flooded the wood and fabric. It was very gingerly that I glided down, expecting the wings to carry away; my next breath was taken when the wheels touched the ground.

We fitted a new plane, took precautions against similar discomfitures, and on the 5th September I started up river in the first Spad. The turn of speed was excellent, but the heat in the pilot's seat was that of a Turkish bath. I got down at Amara with no water left. After a spell of fever she made one sick, for one was not up to it, so I left her there till the temperature might drop, and trundled comfortably on to Baghdad in an old B.E.

While I had been away air reconnaissance had reported the Turks constructing a position S.W. of Shahroban. General Maude, to secure his right flank, decided to eject them, for the Russians had gene. Columns from Baqubah and Beled Ruz marched on the night of the 18th/19th August, and, giving little opposition, the enemy retired into the Jebel Hamrin on the 20th. The weather conditions prevented any further advance. We were as we had been before the arrival of the Russians in April. On August 29th two B.E.s closed with an enemy two-seater over Kizil Robat. Page was doing escort, and saw the right-hand main strut of the enemy shot away. Pursuit was impossible owing to shortage of petrol.

On the 12th September a welcome relief was at last caused by a sudden drop in the temperature to 113 deg. Fahr., as a result of which No. 63 Squadron took a new lease of life.

By this time a track fit for motor-transport in dry weather existed the whole way from Busrah to Baghdad; marching-posts, with tents, fuel, and guard, were situated at convenient intervals. The first convoy of the new motor-transport accomplished this journey in eight days; of twenty-two light tenders one broke down and had to be left at a post. The route was a severe test, deep and sandy, and wide detours into the desert were often necessary to avoid *nullahs*; also escort, rations, and fuel for all the cars was no mean load to bring over the four hundred miles.

With the cooler weather No. 63 Squadron commenced to blow into Baghdad in their new R.E. 8 aeroplanes. With them arrived Mac, who had left us a year before. He came in the role of liaison officer from England, France, and Palestine, with useful information of new methods adopted in those more prominent spheres. He only stayed a week, and then this cheerful soul blew on to India and East Africa. He said that returning to the happy family in Mesopotamia was like returning home. Major-General Hoskins also arrived in an R.E. 8, to take command of the 3rd Division.

The aerodrome at Samarra had been enlarged, and hangars, workshop, store, and dark-room dug-outs excavated by the 1st Corps. It had been decided that the new squadron should be located on the Tigris line; and of 30 Squadron, two Flights on the Diala and one on the Euphrates.

On the 12th September Lieutenant Page was forced to land

behind the enemy's lines near Kifri. Lieutenants West and Dickinson were in company, and landed near Page, who had by this time burnt his machine. Arab horsemen were galloping down as Page ran for the other aeroplane. The old B.E. and its unaccustomed load of three waddled off the ground just in time, and got down safely at Shahroban, Page half-standing on the lower plane with one leg in the front seat.

On the 13th two machines were sent to fly over the sacred city of Kerbela, where Arab demonstrations of doubtful tendency had been taking place. It was thought that the presence of English eyes and the latent threat droning over their city would quieten the multitude. Unfortunately one of the machines had engine trouble, and was forced to land outside the town. To their surprise and relief the occupants were greeted in a friendly fashion by the Arabs, some of whom even craved a "joy ride"! Kerbela is the shrine of Hussein, son of Ali, and grandson of the Prophet; here he and his family were slain in the year 680. It is a place as holy to the Shiahs as Mecca is to the Sunnis.

General Maude, with the first break in the weather, decided to go for Ramadi and wipe out the failure of the last attempt, made abortive by the heat. The Turkish garrison had been consider- ably reinforced, but the prize was the greater. By starting to hammer the enemy again at the first opportunity it gave us the initiative, and it was the Euphrates line down which big movements might be expected. He must not be allowed to rest, or given time to concentrate within striking distance on that line. It was barely the end of summer when we were at it again, hammer and tongs.

Throughout the hot months the Royal Engineers had performed prodigious achievements. In addition to the heavy work entailed to keep the river within its bounds, they had organised Arab and Kurd labour corps, to supplement those from India. Hundreds of miles of light railways had been torn up in India and despatched to Mesopotamia, so that a line was now nearly through between Kut and Baghdad and on to Baqubah. Another metre-gauge was also half-way across the desert to Felujah. The railway tracks thus radiating to all three fronts from Baghdad greatly enhanced the rapidity with which it was possible to strike in force on any single one, and placed the British Force on strong interior lines. Rolling-stock and personnel for these railways poured out from India. The bulk of the river fleet was concentrated between Kut and Amara, on the more navigable section, leaving as much as possible to the railways between Busrah-Amara and Kut-Baghdad. This also greatly reduced the time for the journey between Front and Base. The services of the force were nearly doubled. Specially designed paddle and hospital boats had arrived from England, and the familiar sight" of L.S.W.R. locomotives dragging supplies up to Samarra reminded one of other days and the milk train back to Pirbright or Aldershot.

The 25th September was a black day for the R.F.C. Two of the new R.E. 8's, with the most experienced and enthusiastic pilots, the advanced party of No. 63 Squadron, failed to return from reconnaissance. It was a bitter blow; at last some of the new squadron had got up river, and I had hoped they would build up quickly and form into line as a unit, for there was much work to be done and the new Hun machines must be downed. But almost on their maiden flight the first two are lost. From deserters it appeared that four fast enemy scouts had pursued the R.E. 8's north of Tekrit.

In the engagement that followed one of the R.E. 8's was damaged, and had to come down. Landing on ground which appeared to be clear of enemy, the second machine had followed down to rescue the two occupants of the first, but had been immediately surrounded and fired on by Turks, who emerged from *nullahs* and dug-outs. One of our machines was reported to have been burnt, and the second partially burnt, before being captured. The Turkish commander courteously sent in a letter under a white flag to our advanced troops near Samarra, stating that the pilots and observers were uninjured. They were Captain J. R. Philpot, M.C.; Lieutenant M. G. Begg, M.C.; Lieutenant E. N. Baillon; and Corporal Grant. It was cruel luck; they had just arrived. Poor Philpot, a most magnificent, cheerful, devil–may-care fellow, with a wonderful record from France, eventually died of disease in Turkish hands.

On the same morning that these machines went missing, three Martinsydes from Baqubah destroyed three separate Arab camps south of Baghdad. They were bombed and machine-gunned from an altitude of 500 feet.

By September 26th General Brooking had concentrated his force at Mahdij, fifteen miles above Felujah, on the Euphrates. Merton's Flight also moved up to Mahdij, sixty miles from Baghdad; the only means of communication was by light lorries over a desert track, part of which was barely passable for these vehicles. With ten cars they took stores and spares for a fortnight, and 160 lb. tents for shelter during the daytime. A small power plant was moved out in one of the lorries to keep their accumulators charged for wireless work. The photographic section established themselves in an Arab house at Felujah, and exposures were flown back to be dealt with there, the results being returned forward either by air or despatch rider.

Everything was done to make Ahmed Bey, the Turkish commander, expect our advance up the left bank of the river. The road from Felujah runs up the right bank, but a pontoon bridge was thrown across at Mahdij, and roadwork undertaken on the other side. Troops and dumps were also so disposed on the left bank to complete the bluff; Arab informants were no doubt running to Ramadi with the valuable information.

On the 27th the last series of photographs of the Turkish position had been taken and were distributed to the troops that night before they marched off under cover of darkness. Four miles east of Ramadi the Mushaid ridge, a sandy cliff-like contour, runs north and south; its northern end slopes down to the desert before meeting the river, to the south it slopes to the brackish Habbaniyeh Lake.

The enemy held an advanced position along the crest of this ridge facing east. Their main position was dug about a mile from the town, along the Habbaniyeh Canal, and then refused

Sketch Showing Action at Ramadi

east across sand dunes to the Azizieh Canal. Ramadi was thus strongly protected from east round to south, and by the river on the north. The Turk can have feared little from the desert flank; it meant a long detour from the river, and the water in the Habbaniyeh was salty and unfit to drink. They, however, did not reckon with the Ford car. Therein lay the secret to success. The plan was to work round the southern end of the Mushaid ridge, secure the dam crossing over the Habbaniyeh Canal, and attack Ramadi from the south, where it would least be expected. Arrangements had been made to water the force by Ford vans from the Euphrates. With the crossing of the Habbaniyeh Canal secured, the cavalry brigade were to ride west to the Azizieh Canal, where water would be found, and then "burn their boats" and get behind the enemy astride the Aleppo road. It was a bold scheme, so bold that the enemy could barely expect it.

Before dawn the infantry on the left had secured the dam over the canal, and with daylight the Mushaid ridge was heavily bombarded. The enemy retired at once, and as soon as our bombardment stopped put a heavy barrage on the ridge themselves. They must have assumed that we would follow up our bombardment on to this position, for they had the place accurately registered, and it no doubt was a trap. But they wasted their ammunition in blowing up desert, for not a man of Brooking's force went a yard further up the slope. The 12th Brigade, on the right, turned sharp left, and with the cavalry traversed the Turkish front, effectively hidden by the Mushaid ridge.

To cover this movement the left Brigade, to the west of the Habbaniyeh Canal, advanced and attacked the enemy's southern position. The Gurkhas and Dorsets pressed forward over the bare shingle until they could get no further against the accuracy of the Turkish gunners and enfilade machine-gun fire. They lost heavily but hung on, parched by thirst under the killing fire, all the hot day. Meanwhile the 12th Brigade passed in rear of the 42nd, and coming up on the left won a footing on the Azizieh ridge. The Ford vans plied backwards and forwards with water; thousands of gallons were supplied to man and beast.

Merton's Flight kept in touch with the cavalry, and spent a strenuous day co-operating with all arms. Merton himself unfortunately got a bullet through both legs early in the morning, but managed to land safely.

By nightfall we heard that General Holland-Prior's cavalry brigade was across the Aleppo road. The enemy was hemmed in to the south and south-east by our infantry. To the north flowed the Euphrates. Ahmed Bey was trapped. At G.H.Q. there was a buzz of excitement.

The cavalry had taken up an extended position on some high ground five miles to the west of Ramadi; with horse-holders their rifles were few, but they had mounted their machine-guns cunningly, and were strongly equipped with Hotchkiss guns. At 3 a.m. the Turks bumped into the 14th Hussars in the dark, and made a desperate effort to get through. The bursting storms of rifle and machine-gun fire raged till dawn, but the cavalry were still across the enemy's line of retreat; they gave no ground. With daylight the infantry attack was resumed. The Turks turned at bay and counter-attacked repeatedly, but there was no stopping our men now.

The 39th Garhwalis, on the left, caught sight of the bridge carrying the road over the Azizieh Canal behind the town; the only outlet for any wheels from Ramadi. By it was a battery blazing point-blank as they charged for their muzzles. The Turkish gunners served their guns to the end, and died bravely. The enemy were finished; all their defences had been captured and their retreat was blocked.

White flags began to show over mud walls; 2,000 streamed out of buildings and surrendered to the few Garhwalis; Ahmed Bey gave himself up with his staff to the 90th Punjabis. White flags were up everywhere, and a curious silence hung over all; 3,500 prisoners had been taken, thirteen guns, twelve machine-guns, two armed launches, two barges, and a large quantity of arms, ammunition, stores, and supplies also fell into our hands.

I landed close to General Brooking soon after the surrender; the little general was even more cheerful than usual; by superb tactics he had washed the Turkish force off the map; the success had been made possible by the arrangements to supply water to the troops by car, for the days were still hot; but the magnificent ride and stubborn tenacity of Holland-Prior's cavalry was the decisive factor in the achievement of a brilliant plan.

Many of the Turks seemed pleased to be prisoners; only a few cavalry and some strong swimmers escaped by swimming the river. So swift had been the *coup* that Turkish Army Headquarters at Mosul were unaware of the fate that had befallen the Ramadi garrison. The next morning a German aeroplane from the Tigris glided down with the apparent intention of landing outside the town, but must have spotted something strange, for he switched on his engine at the last moment and made off. Vain efforts to start the engine of a Spad allowed the Hun to get clear.

Brooking's clean sweep and the daily drop in the temperature put new life into the British army, rather the worse for the hot weather. Our spirits were good, we began to feel alive again, and looked forward to getting "some move on" to the north, east, and west of Baghdad.

CHAPTER 6

On Three Fronts

For in and out, above, about, below,
'Tis nothing but a Magic Shadow Show,
Play'd in a Box whose Candle is the Sun,
Round which we Phantom Figures come and go.
                                        —Omar.

A British garrison was left at Ramadi, and Ahmed Bey, with his force, was brought into Baghdad. The Flight on the Euphrates returned to Felujah temporarily, where it was easier to supply them. Before embarkation for their places of detention in India and Burma, the captured Turkish troops marched through Baghdad as a demonstration of the might of British arms, and for salutary effect on the disturbing factions ever at work among the populace. The long column shuffled through the streets between the flashing bayonets of Tommy and Sepoy. Their physique was generally good, but their clothes were in rags, and they did not possess a sound pair of boots among them; their tunics and overcoats were German, with the Imperial Crown on the button. The Christian and Persian population thronged the route to revel in the spectacle, but the Mahommedans mainly kept to their own houses, and the women at some points gave way to their curious wailing.

The same day that Ahmed Bay surrendered—the 29th September—the town of Mendali, on our opposite flank, ninety miles north-east of Baghdad, was occupied by our cavalry, who marched from Beled Ruz. The country around being cultivated, the place had been used by the Turks as a source of supply since the retirement of the Russians. A hundred Turkish cavalry, under a German major, fled into the hills on the approach of our column, but lost some men from bombs dropped by two aeroplanes and from our guns. They left behind them three hundred baggage camels and a large quantity of grain and supplies.

The local Sheikhs came in and arrangements were made for the products of the area to be supplied to the British army instead of to the Turks. Mendali was perhaps a greater loss to the enemy than a gain to us. We had the whole of the rich lower Euphrates area to open up and tap for supplies, but the enemy was forced to exist in utterly barren lands, relying on supplies reaching him by way of rafts, known as *killiks*, down the unnavigable waters of the Tigris and Euphrates.

The 13th Turkish Corps about Kifri, away from either river, were dependent on supply by baggage animals. The problem did not merely concern their army, for the whole population for hundreds of miles was starving. Lieutenant Welman, who had the misfortune to be taken prisoner at Kifri a month later, watched the women crawling about "grazing" on the ground wherever there might be a few blades of grass. The streets of Kifri were full of dead and dying; those who remained alive were but living skeletons. As a result, the deserters that came over to our outposts on this front were numerous.

On the 5th October Lieutenants MacRae and Blake, reconnoitring up the Adhaim River, seventy miles N.E. from Samarra, failed to return. Search was immediately made by another R.E. 8 from Samarra and two B.E. 2C.s from Baqubah. The missing machine was located that afternoon by Lieutenants Adams and West, who went down low to investigate; there were Arabs below, and both machines were hit by rifle-fire. Apart from this the ground was too broken to land without crashing. Adams thought he saw the white skins of two officers without shirts, and that one of them waved to him.

It has since transpired that what Adams saw were sure enough the two captured officers. The Arabs had taken most of their clothing and made them drag their machine some distance over the desert, cutting their backs open with *courbashes*. MacRae laughed at one of the most aggressive, and tried to make the others do the same, but the ruffian felled him to the ground with the butt of his rifle. To watch our machines fade away must have been a bitter moment. Intelligence Branch G.H.Q. and political officers took immediate action in doing all that was possible to get these officers back.

Pamphlets offering large rewards were dropped over the locality, and Sir Percy Cox (Chief Political Officer) sent out an influential Arab, who owned land at Bandi-Adhaim. This Sheikh reached the place by motorcar and horseback, only to receive the news that the two officers had been handed over to the Turks on the 6th. On the long journey to Asia Minor the only consideration they received at all was from the German officers they encountered, who helped them as best they could. There seemed a blight on 63 Squadron.

With the increasing shortage of foodstuffs generally, and the growing difficulties of transport by sea, the cultivation of the country was a matter of urgent moment in order to make the army as self-supporting as possible. Once a vast grain-producing area, the land still retains a soil richly prolific provided that irrigation is possible; as the Tommy said: "Spit on it, and something will grow." The only arid districts are those where salt deposits eliminate vegetation.

The enemy, however, were again in occupation of the Jebel Hamrin on both banks of the Diala, and had control of the canals that branch from that river and irrigate the country to the S.W. and S.E. They had interfered with the water supply, and it was necessary to deny them access to the points of irrigation control. For broader strategical reasons it was also necessary that Force "D" should pull her full weight and attack them whenever within reach in order to relieve pressure on the Palestine front. Accordingly, soon after the Ramadi operations, General Maude decided to eject the Turks from the banks of the Diala in the Jebel Hamrin. For these operations one of the Flights at Baqubah moved up to Shahroban.

To endeavour to cripple the hostile air unit before the movements commenced a raid on the Kifri aerodrome was carried out by Lieutenants Skinner, Welman, and Nuttall, in three Martinsydes. Six 122 lb. and twelve 20 lb. bombs were dropped, and then, to ensure effect, these officers emptied their machine-guns from a height of 2,000 feet at the enemy aeroplanes on the ground. It was thought that at least two were put out of action. The raid was boldly carried out in broad daylight, and the Martinsydes were under heavy fire throughout.

Two of them were badly hit. Skinner had a bullet through his petrol tank, and to get away from the Turk he made for the desert, and came down fifteen miles west of Kifri in enemy country. Nuttall and Welman followed him, and the latter came down nearby, though unfortunately with his engine stopped. Meanwhile some Arabs and a Turkish detachment opened fire with a machine-gun from a range of about nine hundred yards. Nuttall, who had had the water connection to his radiator shot away, but was still flying, attacked this detachment with machine-gun fire from the air, and had the satisfaction of seeing several bowl over, while Skinner and Welman set about burning the stranded machine and started off in the other.

All maps and ammunition were saved, but time did not allow for the salvage of machine-guns, as the enemy were closing in rapidly. The damaged Martinsyde finally blew up through the explosion of a 20-lb. bomb. Nuttall, with his water gone, regained our lines at Shahroban, while Skinner and Welman, wedged into the single seat of their machine, got back to Baqubah. These three officers proved an undefeatable trio on many occasions.

The daring of Frank Nuttall knew no bounds, and he was ever a wizard with his engines. We had gone over to France together in the early days of 1914, when the old R.F.C. was a very limited company, and he had joined up with the first rush as a corporal-mechanic.

After two years this New Zealander joined me in Mesopotamia, more cheerful and dauntless than ever. He never went sick, but in the worst heat would resort to an amphibious life and sit for hours of the day in the Diala with his head just above water reading a book under a large parasol. Though shot about on countless occasions, more than once stranded behind the enemy's lines, and out on every raid or night flight, Nuttall's star never failed him. In the war practically every great spirit went west, but Frank Nuttall came through.

On the 18th October, the opening day of operations, a patrol of three Martinsydes noticed two enemy machines leave the Kifri aerodrome, and kept one in view till they overhauled him fifteen miles north of the Diala, at a height of 7,500 feet. Fire was opened at a range of under 200 yards. The Albatross dived for home and outdistanced the Martinsydes, who followed down to a height of 500 feet. The observer in the Albatross fired steadily from his rear gun the whole way down, and, although the Hun must have been knocked about, he got away. These raids put fear into the hearts of the enemy flying unit at Kifri. They were well watched during the operations of the next few days, and never showed themselves over the scene of action, only leaving the ground when any of our machines happened to appear overhead, when they flew round and round the aerodrome until we had gone.

On the 18th troops of the 13th Division from Sindiyeh advanced on Deli Abbas, and drove the Turks back into the hills. That night General Marshall concentrated three columns, one on the right and two on the left bank of the Diala. The plan was to hold them frontally on both banks while two brigades of the 14th Division rolled in the Turkish left flank and the 7th Cavalry Brigade, under General Norton, enveloped their left rear. There was a bridge over the Diala at Kizil Robat.

At dawn of the 19th October the converging movement commenced, and the cavalry were across the Khanikin road, behind the enemy, by 7.30 a.m. But the Turk had not waited for a second Ramadi. He evacuated the left bank during the night, and the last of his troops were across the bridge at Kizil Robat early in the morning. Our aeroplanes engaged him retreating along the Kara Tepe road, and watched him burn the bridge behind him. Some targets were engaged at extreme range and a few prisoners captured. In the evening the enemy left the right bank after slight opposition, and joined the columns retreating towards Kifri. They crossed the bridge at Kara Tepe, blew it up, and again retired out of touch with the British force. The victory was nearly bloodless. The next day the retreating columns were attacked from the air, and panic and dismay beset the worn-out Turks.

During the summer Wing H.Q. had been augmented by Major Grinlinton, as artillery liaison officer; he did much to promote the efficiency of the artillery co-operation. The "old man" had been blown up and gassed on the Somme, and after firing a round a minute for weeks on end in that sphere of chaotic destruction, it must have been a relief to come to the more scattered strife of the desert. In quiet times in our home at Baghdad he would work out horoscopes till two in the morning with amazing accuracy; but when the first shot was fired he would be found rushing round the desert in a Ford van with a wireless operator, orderly, forty-pound tent, and rations for a week, and a glint in his eye foretold some wonderful counter-battery scheme and Hell for the Turk.

Four of us now lived in the house at Baghdad, "Old Man," "Chocolo," Buxton, and myself; P. S., being of another unit, had gone. They were happy days. "Old Man" was an authority on many things, and an efficient mess caterer; after dinner he and "Chocolo" would sing songs and beat an old German piano far into the night "Where the mountains of Mourne flow down to the sea" and "Twa moons in the sky" still echo in my ears. Between operations "Old Man" spent much time absorbing quinine and aspirin on his bed; the sound of the piano, however, would bring him out even in the throes of a fever, and the old song would start again.

"Huxley," the wireless expert, had by now trained seventy operators and organised numerous wireless stations on the front. The R.F.C. helped the Anzac wireless squadron in the Intelligence work for G.H.Q. Before many months this web of desert aerials was doubled, longer distance plant was installed in aeroplanes, and several transmitting ground stations erected at various points.

One hot day a huge man in shirt sleeves, covered from head to foot in dust, broke into my office and introduced himself as officer commanding the Kite Balloon Company. He had arrived direct from Busrah in advance of his company, and a convoy of cars were waiting outside. Three had been dropped with broken axles at various points in the 400 miles, but here he was; where was the war? and it was a "d———d fine picnic." Jensen was a hardy customer; after twenty years planting in the Malay States he abandoned the fruits of his toil on the first roll of the drum in 1914 to fight for his country. Shot down in a flaming balloon on the Somme, he took to his parachute, which the Hun peppered as he drifted down on some trees in No Man's Land; surviving this and several barrages, he got back to our lines. Meanwhile an insurrection broke out in Malaya; home and estates were devastated, yet sunshine radiated wherever he went; the fact of living was good enough for Jensen.

By mid-October the nights had become quite cold, but sickness was still considerable. No. 63 Squadron were sadly deficient; thirty-two of their ranks had already been invalided to India without seeing the front in Mesopotamia; a further thirty were distributed among the hospitals; added to this six of their number had been captured. Of the other squadron and Aircraft Park some had been invalided and many were in hospital. Bill Bayly had been carried off a wreck to India. Nevertheless, compared to the *débâcle* of a month ago, things had appreciated wonderfully.

The Tigris reconnaissance noticed enemy movements south of their advanced position at Daur on the 22nd October. They apparently desired to avoid detection, for this reconnaissance of two R.E. 8's was met and engaged by two Albatrosses over enemy country. Both hostile machines were driven down by Captain Simpson and Lieutenant Jamieson, with Lieutenants Underbill and Taunton. We heard later that one had been crashed and the pilot had both legs broken; the other was reported damaged; 63 Squadron maintained a close watch.

On the 25th October our advanced patrols interfered with the Turks constructing a position eight miles north of Samarra, and drove them back on Daur. General Maude decided to advance and attack at the latter place; the 7th Division accordingly concentrated forward.

On the 22nd a tragedy occurred at Shahroban. Lieutenants Gardner and Leeson were leaving for reconnaissance, when the engine failed after getting off. Gardner, in order to avoid coming down on 3rd Corps H.Q. camp, attempted to turn. He lost control, the machine dived into the ground, and immediately went up in flames. Gardner got clear with slight burns, but Leeson could not be extricated; the petrol tank had exploded, and it was all over in a minute.

Poor Leeson had done brilliant work with the Horse Gunners, and been specially chosen to join us. So young and so gallant, he had already won a D.S.O. in action, and could ill be spared. Perhaps one of our most expert artillery spotters was Lieutenant R. B. Sievier. "Bob" became a wizard with his wireless work; if he was up the guns never failed to hit; with uncanny genius he would control two or three batteries at a time as fast as they could put on their corrections and get into the targets.

On the 30th October Lieutenant Hyslop, of 63 Squadron, left Busrah with a new Spad to join up with 63 at the front. There was a thick ground-mist between Kurnah and Amara. He was heard flying round, apparently trying to land by a post on the Tigris about forty miles south of Amara, but he crashed into the ground in the mist, and was eventually found dead among the wreckage. The next day Captain Ffiske, of the same squadron, flying up river, dropped a wreath on the funeral at Kurnah.

The 23rd Kite Balloon Company had forty casualties through sickness on the way up river, the result of sending unfit men out from England; balloon units at this period of the war were composed of men unfit for the infantry; the shortage of manpower entailed such a procedure for European warfare, but it was false economy for Mesopotamia. By this time we had grown used to disappointments; reinforcements arrived at Busrah meant nothing till they had reached the front; we learnt to work with a nucleus of personnel. A fortnight later No. 51 Kite Balloon Section arrived from Busrah and put up their gasbag as sentinel over Samarra; the other section of the balloon company followed soon after, and went out to Ramadi.

The 1st Corps on the Tigris were now ready to go for the Turk at Daur. Our operations had generally been preceded by an aerial attack on the enemy's air unit on the threatened front. So, on the 31st October, in order to bluff him, three Martinsydes and three B.E.s attacked the Kifri Aerodrome, the opposite front to that on which operations were imminent.

The formation was led by Frank Nuttall. Over Kifri one of the Martinsydes was seen by two pilots to, go down and land on the west edge of the aerodrome and the pilot to get into a *nullah*; a 112 lb. bomb was observed to burst close to the stranded British machine. Meanwhile an enemy aeroplane had climbed to the same height as our machines. He was engaged by Lieutenants Adams and Cox. Adams' petrol tanks were shot through, and he also was forced to land in enemy country. Nuttall followed him down, although under fire from the ground.

With his machine-gun he cleared the neighbourhood, and then landed just as Adams sent his machine up in a cloud of smoke. It was a matter of seconds, and Adams jumped on to the plane of Nuttall's machine before it had come to a standstill. Nuttall, with Adams clinging on, opened his throttle and roared off downhill, pouring bullets into a Turkish detachment, which fled in terror. It was brilliant. Cox, whose radiator had been pierced by a piece of shell, glided for the Diala with engine seized and on fire. Landing in a deserted area, he started to trek for our outposts, eighteen miles distant.

Successfully avoiding several patrols, he regained the British lines at 4 p.m., having done the course in six and a half hours. At noon that day, after Nuttall had brought Adams back, we knew that there were still two Martinsydes missing; one was down at

Kifri, but where was the other? Cox had not yet got back. Two B.E.s first of all went out in search, but discovered nothing; one was attacked out of the sun by an Albatross Scout, which dived and fired one burst, repeated the evolution without firing, and then flew off north.

To quote Lieutenant Dale, the Albatross appeared to be about 100 M.P.H. faster than his own machine. Then Nuttall and Morris went out intent on finding Cox. Armoured cars also scoured the country. Nuttall and Morris eventually spotted the charred remains of Cox's machine, flew back, and landed by the armoured cars near Kizil Robat. In doing this Nuttall unfortunately crashed his under-carriage on the broken ground.

The Turks started shelling them from a 4.2 inch gun across the river, and Morris was blown some yards by a shell and had his foot damaged. They boarded an armoured car and went to Kizil Robat, where the Sheikh was interviewed and requested to produce Lieutenant Cox without delay. But Cox had by this time reached our lines. The two machines were hauled back from their exposed position by the infantry and returned to their aerodromes the next day. It had been an unlucky and expensive raid, but there was little doubt that one hostile machine was destroyed, and the extraordinary dash and contempt of danger with which it was carried out must have left its mark.

Three machines were lost, but only one pilot, Lieutenant Welman. He was hit by a machine-gun bullet in the left forearm, which smashed both bones and severed an artery. Having fainted from loss of blood, the machine glided on by itself; he "came to" when only 500 feet off the ground, and, managing to regain partial control, landed without totally crashing. The Turks lifted him out and laid him in a *nullah* some distance away, so as to be clear of the bombs, which were still bursting on the aerodrome; one, however, fell within fifteen yards, blowing the hindquarters off a Turkish soldier standing guard close by.

Welman spent three days in Kifri, where a Turkish surgeon operated on the wound. Thence he was sent in an open cart to Kirkuk. The nights *en route* were spent in Arab huts of awful filthiness, while black bread and water were only produced at rare intervals. The artery had been badly fixed up, and by the time he arrived at Kirkuk it was necessary to inject artificial blood to keep him alive. Welman spent six months at Kirkuk; the first two in a small guardroom, alone, no one to talk to and nothing to read. For the remaining four months he was removed to the Turkish officers' hospital.

During all this time he lay on his back; food was scarce owing to the state of famine in the country, and he never had more than two of the smallest meals a day; sometimes there was no bread for weeks. He learnt Turkish, which eventually secured him better attention, but the doctors made a sorry mess of his arm. There were four operations, two without anaesthetic, and successions of fainting were the only relief to the pain. For all the six months he seldom had a wash and the hospital clothes he was obliged to wear crawled with vermin. Fortunately he received his kit, which was dropped by our machines at Kifri.

In January Welman heard that Lander was in a German hospital at Mosul, and managed to send him a letter. Later on, in April, he saw three R.E. 8's come over the Hun aerodrome to drop kit belonging to Captain Haight, who had been taken prisoner on another front. Eventually Welman managed to communicate with his squadron through the kindness of a German flying officer who had gained admission to the Turkish hospital. A note was written to Nuttall and dropped over our lines on their next trip. In May, 1918, Welman left Kirkuk for Asia Minor, *via* Mosul; here he met the first people who spoke his own tongue, Lander and Colonel Beazley, R.E.; the latter had just been captured with Lieutenant Edwards, who died of wounds.

The German Flying Corps buried Edwards in the cemetery, and all turned out in their full kit. Lander, Beazley, and Welman sadly watched the earth thrown over their comrade in captivity, while four machines, led by our old antagonist, Captain Schutz, flew over and saluted the grave. It is best not to think of those six dark months spent by Welman in Kirkuk. It was mere chance that in spite of his weak state he did not fall victim to typhus or smallpox which ravaged the enemy troops, and his strength held out though starved and bloodless.

On the 1st November the 3rd Division, from Istabulat, had closed up with the remainder of the 1st Corps at Samarra. The cavalry division were also marched up during the night and lay hidden in *nullahs* during the day. On the night of the 1st the cavalry and 7th Divisions marched north from Samarra. There were eighteen miles to cover, and it was hoped that the cavalry would get round the desert flank of the Daur position before dawn, when the infantry attack would be launched. If all went well we might hem the Turkish garrison to his ground.

All arrangements had been made with 63 Squadron. "Old Man" and I started off in a Ford car with wireless equipment to be with the artillery when the show started. It was a beautiful starry night, but a shivering wind blew across the desert. We had to make a wide detour to the left to get on to a high plateau, where the going was good, and there was no chance of bumping into enemy outposts.

When you have motored all night over desert and the dawn only shows featureless sand, without any landmark, it is easy to be uncertain where you actually are. There was no sound, and we could see nothing. "Old Man" and I felt somewhat foolish; we might have gone too far and even be behind the Daur position; we might be close up to the Turks, or we might be far to the west in the desert. We got out and jumped about to restore circulation and scan the dim landscape with our glasses. The day was just breaking, and it was devilish cold, so we consumed a Thermos flaskful of coffee.

At length, as the light strengthened, we spied the familiar sight of an armoured car moving slowly in the distance like an insect on the desert. We jolted after it, but they were equally glad to see us, for they, too, were lost, and had been roaming about all night. It was decided to move east, which anyway must bring us to the river, whether behind or in front of the enemy. We at length caught sight of our own troops and the guns just coming into action two miles to the east. The cavalry had lost direction,

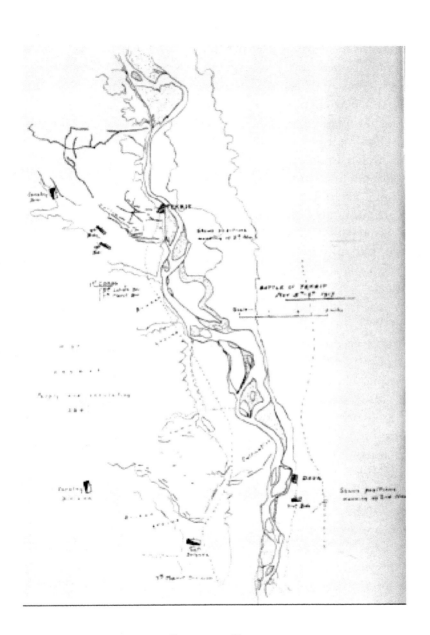

BATTLE OF TEKRIT

also, and had halted some miles from their assigned position when dawn broke, and an aeroplane gave them their bearings. The enemy, however, did not wait; in a night the British army had come twenty miles, and threatened to envelop him. I had a splendid view of the whole situation in the plain below from the top of a *kopje*, where the guns were in action.

The aeroplanes were sending down targets as fast as the Turk got out of his trenches and rapidly retired. The cavalry rode in from the left in an endeavour to cut them off, but immediately they debouched on to the open plain the Turkish gunners got the range accurately. As the regiments trotted down from the high ground and deployed in the open it was more like some field day at Aldershot than actual warfare, until the white, woolly puffs of bursting shrapnel started playing over the top. They were forced to take cover, and the enemy got away north to his Tekrit position.

We had failed to envelop him, but, thanks to rapidity of movement, had captured a very strong position with few casualties. After twenty-four hours' marching and fighting, in which the troops had covered thirty miles, they lay down and slept till the night, when the pursuit was continued towards Tekrit.

By the 4th the 1st Corps and cavalry division were concentrated near the town; the Turkish position was strong and dug in a semicircle, with both flanks on the river; 63 Squadron maintained close contact with the enemy, keeping Corps, Divisional, and Brigade Headquarters continually informed of the situation by message bags. The cavalry, working on the western flank, required their position to be frequently given to them and direction corrected.

The enemy attempted to stop this aerial co-operation by sending out two Albatrosses from Tekrit, but although on each occasion the action was indecisive owing to the jamming of the Spad's machine-gun, the work was never interfered with. All the autumn we experienced many disappointments due to the jamming of these machine-guns. The interruptor-gear of the guns firing through the propeller was new, and it took much experience to adjust them till perfect tune was arrived at. Also the special aircraft ammunition had not yet reached us; the ordinary ground ammunition was a sure source for jambs. Time and again a scout pilot would get right in at a Hun, p–p–pop and the gun would stop, just as the pilot imagined he had his enemy cold in a racing dive on his tail. There was nothing left to do but break away for home and trust he would not follow. Such a crisis in the mad whirl of an aerial battle was more than a bitter disappointment.

On the morning of the 5th November the 8th Brigade of the 3rd Division, "the Fighting Starving Eighth," assaulted the enemy's centre; the 59th Rifles and 47th Sikhs took the first line of a maze of trenches. The enemy counter–attacked heavily; the 124th Baluchis and Manchesters followed in, and a bloody onslaught went on till the afternoon.

The cavalry meanwhile contained the enemy to the west of the town and awaited their chance. This came when the Seaforths and 125th Rifles were launched in under a barrage on the left of the 8th Brigade, and the enemy in front of them gave way. The 13th Hussars and 13th Bengal Lancers advanced at a trot and broke into the charge. This was the second time that Colonel Richardson led his Hussars at the gallop against enemy trenches. Wounded in the charge at Lajj, he had returned from India in time to repeat the performance at Tekrit. The cavalry thundered over the trenches and carried on half a mile beyond.

The Turk fled in dismay, and was caught by the sabres. But the inevitable happened, and the two regiments came under a galling artillery and machine-gun fire. They fought their way back dismounted, but many a trooper and *sowar* was left on the field. Under the smoke and dust of the conflict the Turks retreated north, burning their ammunition dumps as they went, and during the night our patrols entered Tekrit. The enemy casualties were estimated at two thousand.

The Turks were now out of striking distance, and as it was impossible and of no advantage to maintain a large force at Tekrit, the 1st Corps marched back to Samarra, while the enemy took up a position of great natural strength on high rocky ridges astride the river about Fatah, seventy miles north of Samarra.

On the evening of 17th November General Maude was taken violently ill at his residence in Baghdad. Cholera had been prevalent in the town since the cold weather, but although it and smallpox had claimed a good number of victims there was no regular epidemic, the cases being frequent but scattered. This made the problem of segregation all the more difficult for the medical authorities.

On the 17th the general and his personal staff had attended a school treat in the town and drunk coffee, the usual ceremonial custom of the East. The following morning, on the way to my office I learnt that the G.O.C. was dangerously ill and that cholera was suspected. However, a fair percentage of cholera cases had been pulled through, and the doctors were hard at work fighting for his life. Alas, it was of no avail, and the great general succumbed to the violence of the attack at six o'clock that evening.

This sudden blow was a terrible shock to the British army in Mesopotamia, for we had grown to love our chief. My own work had brought me into constant contact with him, as he made a habit of giving me his requirements and discussing all matters with regard to the air personally. He was a leader for whom one worked not only one's hardest but a little bit more. It is that little bit more which can be got out of men only by certain individuals; it is not there and cannot be forced, but it is somehow achieved when the labour is not only one of duty but one of love. F. S. Maude was such a man. He possessed a detailed knowledge of every branch of his profession, for he had spent his career as a student of military matters, and for years had worked hard to attain this end.

It is difficult to define charm, but perhaps in his case it lay in the complete elimination of himself in the scheme of things and, above all, in his naturalness. There was something akin to the schoolboy in his enthusiasm and happiness. It was difficult to get to know General Maude, but once one did it was perfect to work for him. His achievement in Mesopotamia was remarkable, for he had taken on what might almost have been called a hopeless task. Failure after failure and a ravaging climate had depressed the troops. Considerable incompetence prevailed; to the casual observer on arrival the main idea seemed to be to get out of the country. Maude fought it down, and gradually, even to the lowest rank, the call of duty to make the best of it overrode all else. Things were reorganised, and from the root the fabric was reconstructed; but it took time and immense energy from all. The authorities across the sea at last questioned when the Expeditionary Force would attack; but Maude heeded not, and answered "When I am ready."

Lesser men would have started sooner—and failed. Once he had thrown down the gauntlet he never left off; after long weeks of fighting on the Hai one looked at him and wondered if he had failed, but his calmness and patience bred confidence in all, and the force continued hammering and dying cheerfully, till a master-stroke eventually wrought the collapse of a bewildered enemy worn down by our long offensive. He led the troops himself; G.H.Q. had never moved beyond Busrah, three hundred miles behind the army; but when Maude had finished with his work at the Base he left it for good.

He was often too far to the front; at Sinn his advanced G.H.Q. was in front of the 1st Corps at Sannayat; during the pursuit his river-boat was generally close up behind the cavalry; commanders, annoyed to see the G.H.Q. ship passing them, pressed on. At Bawi it had been difficult to persuade the general to stop when the Turkish shells were falling in the river a mile ahead. The smell of powder was too much for him. Apart from professional acquaintanceship I came to know the general privately as far as it was possible for a junior officer to know his C.-in-C.

To dine at his mess was always delightful, and on all occasions there was a very bright spark of humour which would force itself to the fore. In the hot weather he tried himself sorely, for throughout the day he never left: his desk, an evening ride with his *aides-de-camp* being his only diversion. With a quaint disre-

SIR STANLEY MAUDE
TURKISH PRISONERS IN BACKGROUND

gard for weather conditions, the tall figure of the G.O.C. would be seen in home-service khaki and Norwegian boots, when all others were as sparsely clad as possible.

And so the great general passed. It seemed hard that he should not live to receive the rewards that must have been waiting. He died at his post having won the campaign, a brilliant servant of his country, .and lies buried among his soldiers in the British cemetery just north of Baghdad.

The command devolved on Lieutenant-General Sir W. Marshall, of the 3rd Corps, which was taken over by General Sir R. G. Egerton. Brigadier-General Thompson was given command of the 14th Division.

The Turkish aerodrome on the Tigris was now situated at Humr, behind the Fatah position. On 19th November, the day of General Maude's funeral, two enemy machines were reported over our lines from Kifri. They probably had received news of the death of the general, and perhaps were out to seek any signs of a funeral parade. Two successive barrage patrols were sent up, and Nuttall, Cox, and Morris all had engagements. Cox met a Hun only six miles north of Baghdad.

The enemy turned away, and a running fight ensued at close quarters; after a forty-mile chase Cox ran out of ammunition over Shahroban, and had to break off the battle. His Spad had two mainspars, aileron control, and centre section strut shot through, and the Hun must have suffered at least as much. Nuttall, about an hour and a half later, met another over Sindiyeh and chased him to Deli Abbas, when Morris appeared. Unfortunately Morris failed to see Nuttall's machine, and attacked independently, but had to cease fighting, his gun jamming after sixty rounds. Nuttall followed up, chasing the Hun down to below 1,000 feet over Kara Tepe, where he lost him in a ground mist. Several other machines patrolling in their areas sighted 'the Huns, but being slower types could not compete.

British influence had gradually penetrated south into the dark and little-known country between Hilla and Nasiriyeh. They were the rich lands of Mesopotamia, and every acre opened up meant so much more grain for the Expeditionary Force. The inhabitants were of independent thinking, and had ever been a thorn in the side of the Turk. Within reach of the holy cities of Kerbela and Nejef, they were fanatically religious.

Nejef, the shrine of Ali, son of the Prophet, is nearly as holy as Kerbela, the shrine of the martyr Hussein, grandson of the Prophet, which to the Shiah is more sacred than Mecca. Nejef is also a great seat of religious learning, and stores untold treasure in the vaults of the tomb of Ali. It is a city of the dead, for here the Faithful come to die, or are brought after death on donkeys or camels, sometimes long journeys from the other ends of Asia, so that they may lie in peace near the hallowed remains of Ali; the desert around is a mass of graves, while the houses within the walls are the tombs of the wealthy.

It is by far the most romantic-looking spot I have ever seen. After a hundred-mile flight south from Baghdad one came upon this amazing city, packed in a congested mass within encircling walls, and situated six miles west of the Euphrates. Its walls seem the end of all things human; to the north, south, and west there is nothing; you look to the rim of the horizon; on the east only, after a margin of desert flows the Euphrates. Out of the mass rises the huge golden dome of the Mosque; forty miles away it catches your eye like a heliograph through the haze. There are no trees, not a vestige of green round Nejef: just this flashing jewel set in the dark mass of the city abruptly outlined by its wall against the colourless infinity of desert. A track leads in from the Euphrates, and a track goes south a thousand miles over the horizon to Mecca.

Early in the war the persecuted people of Nejef and Kerbela had risen up and ejected the Turks. The Turks thereupon shelled their holy places; this will never be forgotten, but the Arabians held their own till Ottoman menace was banished forever by the fall of Baghdad. It can be understood that intrusion by the British was equally distasteful to these virile folk, and it required the work of such men as Leachman to prove our attitude. The life of an Englishman was not worth much in Nejef, but Leach-

Nejef

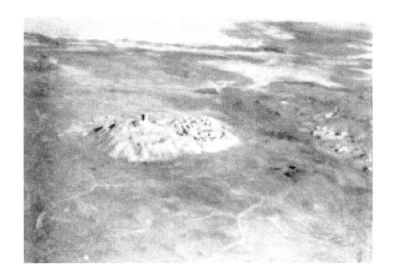

Tower of Babel

man went there alone and returned unscathed. Two aeroplanes flew round the town with a political officer as passenger. From 2,000 feet the inhabitants could be seen running in great alarm to their mosques. Indescribable terror and confusion was caused; a woman was seen to rush at a wall and claw it fiercely when she found she could not scale it. The object was purely demonstrative, and the machines flew away again. It is well to display power to the Eastern mind before negotiating. Good English blood was yet to flow ere Nejef abandoned its hostility.

For the remainder of November the Force continued making good its losses and building up reserves of ammunition and stores on the three fronts. The Supply Services kept the river transport continuously moving between the base and Baghdad; the army was strung out and its communications were long; to maintain a margin of stores seemed a colossal task, and the day's ration for each man by the time it reached Samarra was estimated to cost over one pound. It was an expensive war. The squadrons, in spite of losses, were gradually building up towards full establishment in men and material, a condition which was never reached.

The requirements of the mapping section were inexhaustible; on the Kifri front alone two Flights of 30 Squadron produced just short of 5,000 photographs in the last week of the month. The railway to Baqubah was extended to Shahroban, which relieved the motor transport. Ford convoys were arriving in the country, more armoured-car squadrons, and a new cavalry brigade were under formation, and a complete ambulance train for the Samarra railway had been brought up river on barges from India.

The enemy were out of striking distance on the Tigris; on the Euphrates they occupied Hit; on the Diala they held Kara Tepe and the passes of the Jebel Hamrin on the right bank of the river. Here they were again within rapid striking distance, and General Marshall accordingly decided to attack them, for the third time on this ground. The plan was to force the passage of the Diala against the enemy's left, and at the same time penetrate the Jebel Hamrin towards the Sakaltutan and Zenabil Passes. Concurrently with this operation the cavalry division, under Major-General Jones, were to advance up the Adhaim River, away to the north-west, and get astride the enemy's rear, thus preventing him either from returning or being reinforced from the direction of Kirkuk. Apart from the move of the cavalry up the Adhaim, there were four converging columns.

A volunteer force of Cossacks under General Bicharakov had made their appearance from the mountains of Persia. With 'the revolution the Russians had melted away to their homes in the Caucasus, but Bicharakov and his men, being royalist to the core, preferred to pursue their profession as soldiers of fortune in the cause of the Allies to returning to their distressful country. Colonel Leslie was Chief of the Staff to Bicharakov; in spite of his name he was a Russian, and knew not a word of English or French. A genial old boy, of gigantic proportions, he was descended from Scottish ancestors.

This fact we were not allowed to forget. He came down to Baghdad, and we lunched one very hot day aboard the *Mantis*. Buxton produced a wonderful repast, thoroughly appreciated by our friend, who put away vast quantities, and in spite of the sun washed it down with flagons of *crême de menthe*. Between refills he would get up and toast the Czar, the latter Emperor having already been deposed; revolution being rife in Russia. After wonderful barbaric orations, and having drunk our healths in turn, he would again wedge his huge body into a chair with a sigh and assure us that he only lived for the day when he could retire to his native Scotland!

I expected him to subside with heat apoplexy every minute. The Cossacks, with Corps Cavalry, were to cross the Diala on our extreme right and work round the enemy towards Kara Tepe, an infantry brigade on their left to cross near Kizil Robat and march on Kara Tepe, and a brigade to attack each of the passes in the hills on the enemy's front and right. It was a converging movement of extreme width; there must have been fifty miles between the cavalry division on the Adhaim and the

Cossacks on the Diala. Prior to this, on the night of the 30th November, Lieutenants Skinner and Morris raided the enemy's aircraft at Kifri by moonlight. Due to ground mist little result was attained.

The two Flights of 30 Squadron from Baqubah moved twenty miles up the Diala on the 2nd December to Qalat-Mufti, where General Egerton's Corps H.Q. were established. One Flight, from 63 Squadron at Samarra, had flown to Akab, at the mouth of the Adhaim, to work with the cavalry division. An advanced ground was established at Chai-Khana, thirty-five miles up the Adhaim, where the cavalry left a detachment as guard, and machines could land and gain touch with their H.Q. Wireless was the only means of communication with the cavalry.

On the night of 2nd December the game started. No Hun had been out to watch our movements, and the possibilities were great. At 4.30 a.m. on the 3rd our right-flank troops, the 35th Brigade, forded the Diala three and a half miles above Kizil Robat, and at 5 a.m. the 40th Brigade, our leftmost troops, penetrated the hills two miles north-west of Suhaniyeh, opposite the Sakaltutan Pass. At dawn the attack commenced all along the line. Opposition had been nil, and the enemy were apparently surprised. The resistance was feeble and our progress continuous but slow, owing to the intricacies of the hills. To the north the enemy flooded the country in front of the 35th Brigade, which delayed them considerably. On the right flank the Cossacks crossed the Diala at Kishuk. On the left the 40th Brigade trapped two field guns, and some prisoners in the broken ground. By nightfall the enemy was still holding the Sakaltutan Pass with infantry and two guns, but this appeared 'to be the only point held by the Turks south of Kara Tepe.

On the Adhaim the cavalry division were held up by a strong Turkish force, who opposed the passage of the Jebel Hamrin, in the hills about eight miles east of Bandi-Adhaim. This was unfortunate, as the cavalry were frustrated in their plan of getting astride the enemy's communications, and their role developed into a containing action.

Operations in Jebel Hamrin, December, 1917

During the night of the 3rd the enemy evacuated the Sakaltu-tan Pass, and retired beyond Kara Tepe. Throughout the 4th we continued to follow up. The Cossacks and our cavalry detachment occupied ground about four miles north-east of Kara Tepe, and stopped all traffic on 'the Kifri Road. Air reconnaissance reported the enemy in position on high ground just north of the town, and the bridge over the Nahrin river at Nahrin Kupri blown up. At 4 p.m. the enemy attacked the Russians, but was repulsed by machine-gun and shell fire. On the 5th the 35th and 40th Brigades passed through Kara Tepe, and, supported by artillery, captured the position; the Turks, screened by the hilly country, fled towards Kifri and along the Abu Alik Road.

Offensive air-patrols were out all the time, but enemy aircraft were inactive. One Albatross only got off the ground at Kifri, but did not attempt to climb and attack our machine. "Anzac" prevented two guns from coming into action by attacking the gun teams with his machine-gun. The horses broke loose and stampeded. He afterwards reported that the Kifri coal mine was burning, having been blown up by the Turks. The cavalry detachment pursued as far as Ibrahim Samin, but becoming out of touch and without sustenance further pursuit was abandoned the next day. We buried eighty-seven Turks and made two hundred and fifty prisoners. The British losses were slight in comparison.

The cavalry division remained held throughout at the Bandi-Adhaim defile, the Flight of 63 Squadron being actively employed bombing and machine-gunning the enemy. One column of thirty horse vehicles had been scattered and hunted down in all directions.

The artillery co-operation with Colonel Lynch-Staunton's Horse Artillery Brigade was carried out in quick time. Lynch-Staunton, the keenest of gunners and finest of pig-stickers, had made a hobby of rapid practice with aeroplanes, and brought it, like everything else he did, to a fine art. His wireless station could come into action in ninety seconds. "V" Battery won a case of beer, promised to the battery that scored the first direct hit. A fine soldier and sportsman, "Lynch" fought in Mesopotamia for nearly three years, winter and summer without ceasing, only to be killed in action a few days before the Armistice, and he had made such plans for shooting and polo and leave to England!

On the 8th December the troops were withdrawn, leaving detachments in the Sakaltutan and Abu Zenabil Passes, while a bridgehead was constructed at Kizil Robat. The next day patrols went forward to occupy Khanikin, on the Kirmanshah Road. Air reconnaissance reported the enemy streaming along the Kirkuk Road and Kifri abandoned, the coal mine still burning.

Doubtless puzzled by our withdrawal from Kara Tepe, Ihsan Ali sent aircraft over the Diala four times. Thrice they dodged our patrols, but on the 13th December Skinner and Cox, on two Spads, closed with a big two-seater at 9,000 feet above the Adhaim River. In accordance with a prearranged plan, Cox had climbed another thousand feet higher than Skinner, so that he would be spotted first by the Hun. Meanwhile Skinner got into position underneath and brought his top machine-gun to bear. Cox dived on the enemy six times out of the sun, but his gun kept jamming with faulty ammunition. Skinner, only fifty feet below the Hun, got in twelve rounds, but his gun also jammed. and the Hun escaped. But for the infernal jams he was a dead bird. The two pilots came back "sick unto death."

The following document, captured in the Kara Tepe operations, was interesting:—

To the Commandant of the 156th Regiment.

In order to deceive the aeroplanes from the time that they are in sight, the infantry battalions which are at Kara Tepe along with the first battalion of the 156th Regiment, which is at the south of Nahrin, will at once take the road toward Jebel Hamrin without waiting for an order, without striking their tents or taking their packs. They will continue their march till the aeroplanes have disappeared, and will rest at 'the place where they will have arrived. If the aeroplanes are returning, the battalions will continue their march toward Jebel Hamrin, until they are no longer in sight, and then will return to their own camp.

The gunners, along with the machine-gunners, will fire at the aeroplanes without waiting for orders.

Acting Commander of the 6th Division.

Kaynimre Kain,

Mimamad Amin.

It was an old ruse, and we knew it well.

On December 5th, while the battle at Kara Tepe was in progress, "Intelligence" at G.H.Q. received information that a convoy of a hundred and sixty camels was moving from Humr on the Tigris across the desert to Hadithah, on the Euphrates. Their probable position was worked out accurately, and Captain Simpson and Lieutenant Caldwell, of 63 Squadron, went out from Samarra to hunt them down.

In the morning they failed to locate the caravan, but a further effort in the afternoon discovered them far out in the desert. The two officers went right down and blew Arabs and horses to glory with bombs and machine-gun fire from a height of three hundred feet. It was an efficient achievement that we could know when and where enemy convoys were at large in the desert, and, although a hundred and eighty miles from Baghdad, could stretch out our arm to the exact locality and blot them immediately.

In the middle of December the weather broke. We had had no rain for a year, but high southerly winds now brought scudding clouds and torrential showers, which submerged the Busrah aerodrome and turned that at Baqubah into a swamp. It is pleasant after a year again to feel rain in your face when there is a dry house to go to, but out in the desert it is different; one sits shivering while the damp drips through the sun-rotted canvas. Hours spent in the construction of cunning drainage systems are of no avail; they eventually overflow and one's kit floats about in the tent.

At night fearful blasts of wind uproot tent-pegs, and to save the complete collapse of your happy home you rush out to wield a mallet and strain on ropes like one possessed. You turn

KHAZIMAIN WITH RAINSTORM BEYOND

IN THE WAKE OF THE STORM

in again between damp blankets and attempt sleep under every conceivable form of covering. About four in the morning the scared face of a Pathan sentry peers out of the gloom, and by his wild gesticulations and vehement "gibberish" you realise that something is wrong.

Out you go again into the gale, in gum boots and a mackintosh over your pyjamas, in time to see a hangar on the point of collapse. Officers and men are routed out in the darkness to hang on to ropes and save the machine. It is as bad as shortening sail in a breeze at sea. The dawn breaks over flooded wilderness; cold, wet, and feverish, you swallow some sardines, for the cook cannot light a fire except to make a little coffee for breakfast. After a hot weather or so in Mesopotamia the blood runs thin, and one shivers more easily.

For the rest of the month there were no more operations, but with the reinforcements of machines and pilots we began to feel our strength, and determined, in the jargon of the air, "to keep a vertical draught up the enemy." To carry this intention into effect, we worried him in his country whenever a gap in the unfavourable weather allowed it. He seldom retaliated, but did not take his punishment lying down, for on the approach of our machines up would come the little Albatross and Halberstadt scouts to interrupt the raiders.

On the 17th December eight machines of 63 Squadron went out in two formations on a voyage of destruction. The first formation left Samarra at eight a.m., followed twenty minutes later by the second. When the first reached Humr they were attacked by three enemy scouts, speedier and of faster-climbing power. Lieutenants Caldwell and Griffith, in an R.E. 8, were set upon by two of these wasps, and almost immediately had both petrol and oil tanks pierced.

Griffith, while engaging both with his rear gun, was also wounded in hand and arm by the hail of bullets from the Huns. He managed to continue firing till the end of the drum of ammunition, which, however, he was unable to remove. With oil and petrol ebbing fast Caldwell turned his machine for home, eighty miles distant; unaccountably the Huns also broke off the engagement, being probably short of ammunition. Caldwell nursed his engine till it "seized up" only four miles from Samarra. The third Hun engaged two of the remaining R.E. 8's, and kept up a furious attack for 'thirty minutes, when he dived for his aerodrome. Both these machines were knocked about, but got back safely. This resistance was unusual, and prevented the first formation from accurate bombing, but the way had been cleared for the second, who made considerable havoc on the Humr aerodrome.

Without a fighting escort, the offensive in enemy country always lays the bombing machines open to attack by enemy fighting scouts. This must be accepted, unless the distance is sufficiently short for fighting scouts to accompany the bombing aeroplanes to their objective, and unless there are sufficient fighters to do this. The R.E. 8's were only a class better than the old B.E.s as regards offensive work, for which they were not designed. The faster, heavier fighter-reconnaissance type able to protect itself were in use on the Western Front; we on our side-show must wait patiently till there were sufficient to be spared, and meanwhile put our best foot foremost with what we had. We were generally lucky.

On the Diala front the Huns had moved their aerodrome back from Kifri to Tuz Kurmatli, eighty-five miles north from Baqubah. This was bombed by 63 Squadron, but without serious opposition. Nevertheless, these raids were always exciting enough. One set out on a long flight to distant enemy country with all the chances of being stranded in the desert should the engine happen to go wrong. The inhabitants were an uncertain element, with slow methods of putting an end to foreigners. There was always, also, the certainty of a fight on arrival at the objective; and then the long run home, perhaps damaged by German bullets—yes, one had breakfast in (the morning and never quite knew where one would have lunch.

But in war you get accustomed to living from hand to mouth; the present is always cheerful, and the uncertainty of the future breeds a lightness of heart which makes boys of older men.

In Christmas week a German dropped a letter at Samarra, with two others from Philpot and Lander. The following is a translation of that from the German pilot:—

Honoured Sirs and Fellow Sportsmen,—
I am herewith sending you some letters which I have received by bearer. Owing to a mistake they only came into my possession a few days ago, and I therefore request you to excuse the delay.
Further, I have a request 'to make. On 1/11/17, while flying over El Aschik, I lost my *kelpek* (a Turkish officer's cap with flying badge). If it should be found I should be very glad if I could have it back again.
With best wishes.
K. O. Halder, Pilot."
On the back of the envelope was written in pencil:
We are again ready to accept challenges in the air.

The letter from Philpot read:—

Dear Colonel,—Captain Schutz has very kindly undertaken to have this note dropped. We are all well and being excellently treated. Could you have a parcel or parcels dropped containing some 'thick clothes (from Ordnance, if ours have been sent home) for Begg, Baillon, and me? Corporal Grant has been sent elsewhere. Also some money in cash, about £100. If you will write to Cox's they will settle this for me. No parcels or gold allowed out of England for prisoners in Turkey now. Captain Schutz has undertaken to have this parcel safely delivered if you will have it dropped. Begg's extension fell off in the air while we were both diving on a Halberstadt, and my engine never picked up again when I shut off to help him. I am so sorry. Goodbye. With best wishes to all.
I remain, Yours obediently,
J. R. Philpot, Capt. R.F.C.
PS.—Also, if possible, some chocolate or tobacco.

This was the last we heard of Philpot.

And so another Christmas came round; it was perhaps more gay than the last, for the flesh-pots of Baghdad were of greater resource than those of the desert, and many officers were given leave for a few days from the Fronts.

Humr was again bombed on the night of the 27th, and a large formation of fourteen machines from both squadrons mopped the place up on the 28th. Two Halberstadts were encountered during the bombing. The first followed for three minutes at a distance of two hundred yards, but on coming under the concentrated fire of three R.E. 8's dived away, and preferred to land on the aerodrome among the bombs. The second Hun took six drums of Lewis gun-fire, and was driven on to the ground near the junction of the Lesser Zab and the Tigris. A cluster of four enemy machines was found outside a hangar; these and the hangars were plastered with bombs. All pilots and observers agreed that they must have been destroyed. At one particular moment eleven bombs were seen to burst simultaneously around and among the enemy aeroplanes. The rear of the formation, under Captain Everidge, was unable to see the ground for smoke of bursting bombs and fire coming from the hangars.

All that the enemy could muster in reply to this were two machines, which bombed the camp of 63 Squadron at Samarra, at the stroke of midnight on the last night of the Old Year. To quote Major Bradley, commanding 63 Squadron:

We had a good doing last night by the Huns. The waiter was just heralding in the New Year on an empty shell case, and I was proposing the health of all in a glass of stout, when they came over. They made very good shooting; one bomb twenty yards from my pony, one near 'A' Flight mess, another ten yards from the motor transport park, and one by the cookhouse door, which destroyed our cookers, 'dixies,' water-carts, etc., and nearly got some N.C.O.s in a trench. A large piece of bomb went through the orderly-room tent. Altogether a pleasant New Year's evening.

This was too much, so on the 3rd January we attacked Humr again, twelve strong, and put seventy-nine bombs among them. The Huns were out to stop us, and three combats took place over the aerodrome. Lieutenant Jacks and Corporal Huxley were singled out by three scouts, above, behind, and below. After fifteen rounds from the Corporal's gun the enemy astern went spinning down into the clouds, apparently out of control, and the other two veered off. Two other R.E. 8's had brushes with 'the enemy, who, however, would not close. Page had a forced landing twenty miles from home, but was located by a search machine, and rescued by armoured cars, who remained out all night, and towed the aeroplane back on the following day.

On New Year's Day our wireless station picked up the following message, faint but clear, from the Eiffel Tower:—

> *Journée marquée seulement par de vives actions d'artillerie en Champagne, dans la région des Monts et sur la rive droite de la Meuse, dans le secteur de Bezonvaux. Pas d'action d'infanterie. A tous nos Alliés et amis nous addressons nos meilleurs souhaits de Bonne Année.*

Early in the New Year Lieutenant Caldwell met with a tragic death. He started out to rendezvous with two other machines, and was heard of no more. Parties searched the country in vain; it was not till a week later that, acting on Arab advice, his body was found near Daur. There were no signs of violence, but he had been stripped except for socks, which were caked with mud from walking. Medical officers certified that he had died from exposure. Caldwell was found about fifty miles from where it was reported that an English machine had come down. Evidence seems to point that he had evaded the Turks, but fallen into the hands of the Arabs, who had taken all his clothes. The perishing nights and scorching sun by day would not allow a human to go far under those conditions. Another fifteen miles and he would have won back.

Another forced landing, with not quite such disastrous results, befell Lieutenants Mills and Taylor, who burnt their machine

Hun Aviators who burnt their machine at Ramadi

and set off as hard as they could to reach our lines by a wide detour through the desert. Our armoured cars and aeroplanes were scouring the country, so was the Turkish cavalry. Alas, with armoured cars in sight they were caught by the enemy, after having covered thirty miles, a stout effort.

The enemy scored their first direct hit with antiaircraft gunfire during a raid made by twelve machines on the Kifri aerodrome. The machine hit was a D.H. 4, the first of a powerful fighter-reconnaissance type; its occupants, Lieutenant Bean and Sergeant Castor, were blown to atoms at 7,000 feet. The pilot next behind in the formation was suddenly aware of debris in midair; there was nothing left larger than one's hand.

On the 12th, while I was at Felujah, a "Zepp" message reported a Hun coming down the Euphrates from Hit. We were sitting down to lunch in the Flight mess when the orderly came in; there was a general bolt for the aerodrome. My own machine was standing ready, and two others were run out without delay. Not waiting for coats or other gear, Merton leapt in behind me, and we were off the ground within five minutes of the call.

Having gone some miles upriver beyond where the Hun had been reported, and having hunted the air without result, we came back. To our surprise on landing we were met by the jubilant remainder of the Flight with two German officers. Apparently they had watched us pass close underneath the enemy machine soon after leaving the ground. The Huns had seen the three British machines pass to cut them off, and thereupon landed near the aerodrome owing to their engine seizing up. They managed to burn their machine before capture.

It was a cheap victory, for not a shot was fired. The two prisoners were given lunch by their would-be destroyers. Being the flight-commander's birthday it was a good lunch; I remember there was beer and *pâté de foie gras*. The captives had not seen the like since leaving Germany. Both were dour and Hunnish; 'the pilot was very young, he looked about seventeen, and his observer, a grim-looking monster in spectacles, was old enough to be his father. To my surprise the pilot gave the name of Haider, my correspondent of a few weeks back. This was amusing, for I remembered that he had written on the envelope:

We are again ready to accept challenges in the air!

I asked him about his lost *kelpek*, but he explained that that was just a joke. Well, his joke had ended badly. Taking two men as guard, I motored them across the forty miles of desert to Baghdad in the afternoon. We broke down *en route;* it was a curious situation, being stranded in the desert with two foes. They were of course unarmed, and I had a couple of *sepoys* with me; the fifth man was the driver; fortunately we got ahead again. They were our first informants that poor Paddy Maguire, captured a year before, had died of his burns; we also learnt that his opponent had died of dysentery in the summer, and that Lander was still in hospital at Mosul.

On the night of 24th January there was an air raid on Baghdad. This was the first and only time that they bombed the city, although we had long expected them. A system of defence had been worked out, and anti-aircraft guns were situated at various points to co-operate with the searchlights of the gunboats, but they came and went unscathed, only causing a few casualties in a hospital. We decided on a night of persecution as a lesson against any further disturbance of our slumber. From 8.30 p.m. on the following evening till dawn of the 26th our machines harried 'the enemy camps, bivouacs and aerodromes at Humr and Kifri. They left at half-hour intervals through the night and bombed and machine-gunned everything that came in their path. It was a night out for the squadrons, and must have been a night out for the Turks. In spite of the nature of the operation there was only one casualty, and that was the second D.H. 4.

Page, who went out from Baqubah to search in an old B.E., was attacked by a Halberstadt, which he drove off, and returned with a negative report. The two officers in the D.H. 4 were Nuttall and Bob Sievier, both veterans of fame, and a greater loss than we cared to consider. But to our joy they eventually turned up. Turkish bullets had damaged their engine at 1,000 feet, but Nuttall glided down and made a perfect landing in strange country in the dark, his engine on fire. They were two miles N.E. of Kara Tepe, twenty-four miles behind the enemy's lines, and close to his camps. Taking a Lewis gun apiece and the three remaining drums of ammunition they wasted no time in getting clear of the burning machine. Making a detour, they then struck a course by the stars for the Diala. Nuttall and Sievier were thoroughly enjoying themselves.

If only a Turkish cavalry patrol would come along, they intended to wipe it out with their machine-guns and capture the horses to save further walking. Stumbling all night across the broken country they eventually reached the river without being intercepted. But here there was difficulty, for they could get no further, and were still in enemy country. The British bridgehead at Mirjana could not be far off, but watery *nullahs* prevented further exploration. Having come far carrying heavy loads they lay down in a ditch and slept soundly.

Awakened by the hot sun they exposed themselves in order to attract the attention of British outposts on the far bank, and were greeted by a burst of machine-gun fire, which nearly proved their undoing. A handkerchief tied to a reed eventually produced "R. U." signalled from the opposite side. They answered "R.F.C., S.O.S.," then moved within hailing distance, and an armoured car was sent to bring them in. The two officers had really achieved rather a notable performance in covering twenty-four miles in the dark carrying two machine-guns with ammunition, and winning back to our lines.

The inhabitants of North-West Persia were starving, so British posts were extended up the Persian road as far as the head of the Pai Tak Pass to open up the road and improve it for trade and food supplies. Before the end of January we established a landing-ground and petrol-dump at Kasr-i-Shirin, thus enabling two aeroplanes to reach Kirmanshah, a hill town 5,000 feet up and eighty-five miles in from Kasr-i-Shirin. Despatches were brought down from the British Consul there the following day. A message had come through describing the ground in this mountain fastness, and we relied on the skill of the pilots to land on the snow without crashing. It is necessary to start from Kirmanshah before the sun is up, as the heavy frost in the night leaves the snow hard, but immediately the sun rises the thaw makes the ground impossible. The troops camped high up on the road endured many hardships from the cold and shortage of rations, for in bad weather it was difficult to supply them. Living under canvas in the snow, is trying to the human frame after sojourning in the fires of the desert, and we had not gone to Mesopotamia clad for the Arctic.

CHAPTER 7

A Last Crowded Hour

And when Thyself with shining Foot shall pass
Among the Guests Star-scattered on the Grass
And in thy joyous Errand reach the Spot
Where I made one—turn down an empty Glass!
                                        —Omar.

Clouds were gathering over the Caspian in the north, and a phantom army of officers, N.C.O.s, and men from overseas was arriving at Busrah. Volunteers from Mesopotamia and all scenes of war began to accumulate at Baghdad. Australians, New Zealanders, Canadians, and English, they were known as the "Hush Hush Army." We were not allowed to talk about their mission, but we knew that some swashbuckling game was afoot, for they were as tough a looking crowd of cheery customers as our race could produce; veteran fighters all, and a formidable enough gang to back any man into battle.

General Dunsterville, the original of Kipling's "Stalky," arrived to lead them. They were to cut themselves away from Mesopotamia, migrate north through Persia into Armenia, and there muster the Armenians and train them into an army to march against the Turk or Bolshevik, thus securing our threatened right flank. It was a daring enterprise. They faded away over the mountains as silently as they had come.

The situation at Teheran was volcanic; internally there was faction against faction; the power of the Shah was doubtful. There were Germans, Turks, Russians, Swedes, French, Austrians, Americans, British, all living cheek by jowl in this "neutral" capital.

Colonel Stokes, who had been military attaché in Teheran for several years before the war, was ordered to reach the British Legation at that place as soon as possible. A convoy of Ford cars, under Major Sir Walter Barttelot, were making preparations to trek from Baghdad, but would probably take some weeks to get through. Stokes approached me about getting there by air, and we decided it was a practicable, though perhaps hazardous, undertaking. Teheran is seven hundred miles from Baghdad; the course lay over 12,000 feet mountain ranges and wild uncivilised country.

There was no map of any accuracy, and the winding road lost itself among snows and mountain passes. It promised to be a wonderful flight, and one felt a great desire to see this remote capital, situated high up in the mountains hundreds of miles from civilisation, a centre of the intrigue of many nations. But it was impossible for me to go. Browning, who had been with us as observer before the capture of Baghdad and was now a full-blown pilot, was entrusted with the enterprise. Two machines started off, one carrying extra petrol instead of a passenger. They both replenished at Kasr-i-Shirin, and went on to Kirmanshah. Landing at Kirmanshah, one was filled up with the spare fuel from the other, and thus able to negotiate the further three hundred miles to Teheran.

Browning left Kirmanshah in a snowstorm on the morning of the 24th, and climbed to 13,500 feet on a bearing for Asabad. He did not again pick up the ground till near Kangavar, and only just cleared the Asabad Pass. The 19,000 feet peak of Demavand, behind Teheran, was sighted a hundred and eighty miles away, and gave a good landmark.

On arrival at the Persian capital all efforts were made to intern him by the Swedish *gendarmerie*, in spite of the fact that machine-guns and other armament had been stripped from his aeroplane at Kirmanshah, so that he should not violate neutrality. (British, Russian, and Turkish forces had been fighting in

Persia for two years!) But the designs of the Swedes were frustrated by the superior numbers of Cossacks present. A guard of forty was maintained to preserve the machine from destruction. The natives of Teheran could not understand that the aeroplane itself was the means of flight, but thought it only the carriage to sit in, and that the propeller merely acted as a fan to keep the airman cool while he exerted himself with some hidden wings, which they were very intent to discover on the person of the pilot. They examined Browning's flying badge, but pointed out in argument that these "wings" were too small to fly with, and that there must be others elsewhere.

The town was crowded with enemy, particularly Austrians freed by the Bolsheviks from Russian prisons. The German flag flew cheerfully opposite the Union Jack on the respective Legations. The warring nationalities kept sullenly to themselves. The Shah's palace is outside the town; he expressed great curiosity to see the British aeroplane, but did not dare to come into Teheran: there were those who were engaged in starving the population, having appropriated all the wheat in order to put up the price.

Meanwhile Browning awaited the arrival of the Ford convoy, to refill with fuel for the return journey. The time was spent playing poker with Swedes and Russians and their ladies. The night before taking off he received a note from the Shah requesting him to fly over his palace on his return journey. Immediately before starting, however, came another note cancelling the request in case foreign eyes should probe the sanctity of the harem from above. Browning had telegraphed to me, *via* India, that he had landed in a barrack square, out of which it was hazardous work to fly the aeroplane. I had wired back suggesting knocking down a gap in the wall; this apparently entailed the demolition of the Regular Persian Army barracks, and the project was but coldly received by the Legation!

However, he eventually flew out into the open country by emptying the tanks and lightening his machine. Before leaving, Sir Charles Marling insisted that a passenger, who could speak Persian, should accompany Browning in case of a forced

Browning's arrival at Teheran

landing. Their *ghulam* (porter) was accordingly ordered to go, and thoroughly enjoyed the flight to Kirmanshah, where oil and petrol were picked up. From there Colonel Bicharakov, commanding the Russian Partisan Detachment, was brought down to Baghdad. It was a notable achievement; our aeroplanes then were not Handley-Pages or Vickers-Vimy.

In the middle of February another squadron arrived at Busrah, a fighting squadron, under Major von Poellnitz, equipped with the latest machines. Fortunately their arrival was timed more happily than the last, for the weather was still cool, and they came upriver with few casualties from sickness. Two of their Scout Flights were located at Samarra and Mirjana, to attack any Hun that approached our forward positions. The long-distance D.H. 4 Flight remained at Baqubah. Von Poellnitz unfortunately was killed soon after by the capsizing of his motorcar over an embankment. The wing had grown, and now mustered more than a thousand men and a hundred officers.

The marshes of the Euphrates south of Hilla to Nasiriyeh being uncharted, two aeroplanes went to Kufa to carry out a survey of this little-known land. The whole area was in an unsettled state, and troops had been despatched south to protect the isolated political officers and friendly tribes. While flying to Kufa a failing engine forced me to land within a mile of the ruins of Babylon. Armed Arabs commenced to collect at once, and I was glad to see the arrival of a few *shabbanas*, or local levies, organised by the political department.

These *desperados*, on their little Arab ponies, revelling in their authority, set about "knouting" the crowd in a most energetic manner. A Sheikh lent me his pony, and with a *shabbana* as escort, I galloped six miles to Hilla, where there was a British garrison and telegraph wire. The short stirrups and impossible Arab saddle, with only the usual single cord to the pony's mouth, afford no control and cause agonies of cramp to the European. My steed, however, knew the road, and clattered over the rough ground with a wonderful skill and fine turn of speed which, with only my cord, I was quite incapable either of controlling or directing. A breakdown party flew out from Baghdad, and with Durward, the photographic officer, I flew on to Kufa the next day.

While stranded we had a look at Babylon, a mass of half-buried ruins rising in a cluster from the sand. Since 1899 the Germans had been hard at work excavating, and had built a museum by the river. As soon as our influence penetrated as far as Hilla, the military authorities protected the museum, otherwise there would have been little left of it after a few visitations from roving subalterns. Nearly every brick bears an inscription, records of the days of Nebuchadnezzar and prehistoric dynasties, for the Babylonian ruins, as at present seen, have their foundations on previous Babylons. The salient features of the place are the Ishtar Gate, built by Nebuchadnezzar, and a statue of a lion standing over a man.

On the way to Kufa we passed the mound and ruins which Arab tradition regards as all that remains of the Tower of Babel. It has the appearance of a Scottish "doocot," and is certainly a very ancient edifice. These traces of a bygone age, standing by themselves in the wilderness, seemed in their silence to hold aloof from the latest achievements of man; one felt in an aeroplane that one was outraging their sanctity.

We found the two survey aeroplanes in the desert half-way between Kufa and Nejef, guarded by Territorials, and here I met an old friend, Frank Balfour, political officer of this wild district. There had been shooting in the bazaars, and this lonely work among fanatical thousands was no light responsibility. A few days later Marshall, of the Dogras, was murdered in Nejef, and Frank Balfour, besieged in his house, held out until relief arrived. Nejef was blockaded by our troops and thereby cut off from water except for a few brackish wells inside the city.

After a period of siege those responsible were surrendered. A somewhat unfortunate incident took place when I sent a flying officer with important despatches from G.H.Q. to the officer commanding the British column. It was not without humour. The pilot entrusted with the despatches was told to drop them without landing, so on getting into his machine he explained to the mechanic who was accompanying him to throw them over when he waved his hand and pointed down. They set off; on approaching Babylon the pilot thought he would like to point out the ruins for the edification of his mechanic. So he circled round and pointed. Away went the despatches! The pilot arrived back with this sorry tale; there were hectic interviews with the powers, and Indian cavalry searched the area for two days, until the secret papers were fortunately recovered. The pilot and mechanic received their fill of abuse!

I took F. B. over the southern extremities of this district, an area of swampy vegetation thickly populated by marsh Arabs, and then left him at Kufa and went on to Baghdad. A few days later news filtered through of the death of Marshall and the plight of Balfour a hundred miles to the southward. Armoured cars were despatched to his assistance, and aeroplanes went down to cooperate with the column. But, more important still, I possessed a bottle of old liqueur brandy, which the pilot was to deliver, come what might. It reached him.

In the middle of February our eyes were turned towards the Euphrates front. Since the capture of Ahmed Bey at Ramadi there had been no fighting; the resources of the district had been developed, and our influence established among the local tribes. The enemy had, however, reinforced this front, and were concentrated about Hit and Salahiyeh, with his forward troops at Uqbah, between Hit and Ramadi. The railway from Baghdad to Felujah was complete.

The enemy, in considerable strength, were well within striking distance, and General Marshall again decided to take the offensive, and at least eject him from his positions, if not destroy or capture his force. After Ramadi the latter event seemed unlikely. By the occupation of Hit we should also appropriate the valuable bitumen wells, for which the place is famed, and deny him the desert road connecting his Euphrates front with Tekrit, on the Tigris.

On the 19th February a column, under General Lucas, moved

up from Ramadi and occupied Uqbah without opposition. Air reconnaissance reported the enemy to be evacuating their trenches south of Hit and taking up a position on high rocky ground two miles above the town at the Broad Wadi, where gun-pits and dumps were located; two enemy aircraft were at Hit; one in the air refused action and dived for his aerodrome.

A Flight from Baqubah and one from Samarra flew to Ramadi and formed a composite squadron under D. H. for the Euphrates offensive. The transport from Samarra came down to Baghdad by rail and completed the journey by road; there was no suitable road between Samarra and Baghdad; at that time a road meant an unmetalled desert track cleared of boulders and carried by rough bridges over the *nullahs*.

The transport from Baqubah, in spite of heavy rain which made the desert well-nigh impassable, reached Ramadi, a hundred miles distant, in one day; 52 Kite Balloon Section pushed up to the advanced troops at Uqbah, and the next fortnight was spent accumulating supplies, concentrating troops in the forward area, and bombing the enemy. In one week three tons of bombs were dropped and 9,000 rounds fired from the air at ground targets. The Hun aeroplanes on Hit aerodrome received particular attention, and were subjected to showers of bombs at short intervals. One enemy machine was totally destroyed by a direct hit by Lieutenant Berrington, so they moved their aerodrome fifty miles back to Hadithah. Rain and low clouds did much to hamper both aerial work and the movement of transport.

The influence of a German political officer at large in Persia had been causing considerable annoyance. Traps had been laid for him, but the elusive von Drueffel had never been caught. Aeroplanes scoured the country where his presence had been reported from outside sources, and eventually two machines found and bombed his camp. It was later ascertained that six of his wireless operators were killed, but that von Drueffel still lived.

There was still another front for which Force "D" was responsible, at Ahwaz, up the Karun river, far away to the south-east. Here a British garrison had been engaged for the last three years in protecting the oilfields and guarding our flank against the wild Bakhtiari tribes to our right rear. For German influence was rife in Southern Persia. There had again been trouble, and the need of aeroplanes was telegraphed to Baghdad by General Younghusband. Petrol and oil were despatched up the Karun river, and officers who happened to be at Busrah were ordered to proceed there in two new machines from the Aircraft Park.

Unfortunately Captain Parker and Air-mechanic Neilson were killed when starting off on this expedition. Their machine, which was heavily loaded, crashed into the ground from three hundred feet. Two aeroplanes reached Dizful, and with a political officer as observer reconnoitred the disturbed area. They were stranded at Shush by bad weather, but eventually regained Ahwaz and returned to Busrah.

The enemy, becoming uncomfortable at our forward movement and concentration on the Euphrates, left nothing to chance, and evacuated Hit on the afternoon of March 8th. Our troops advanced and occupied the town without opposition on the following day. Flying along the Aleppo road I watched their columns winding back and we managed some execution with the machine-gun.

The country above Hit becomes rocky, and the Euphrates flows down past cliffs and steep banks. As with the Tigris at Samarra, it is the end of the alluvial plain of Mesopotamia. The desert is broken and hilly, as between Suez and Cairo. Captain Haight and Lieutenant Hancock had vanished into it five days previously; search machines eventually discovered the charred remains of their aeroplane two and a half miles N.E. of Hit. A deserter reported that their engine had been damaged by rifle-fire, that the officers had burnt their machine, and were believed to be prisoners.

I landed on the German aerodrome at Hit just as our advanced troops were passing through, and, borrowing a bombardier's horse, caught up the head of the column with my report. Hit stands up from the desert like a mediaeval fortress, the cause

KITE-BALLOON AND ANTI-AIRCRAFT GUN IN THE DESERT

HIT

of this elevation being ruins of former Hits; the town crumbling with decades is built up again on its own ruins, and so, with the passage of time, it climbs up above the surrounding country. It was the same with Babylon. Hit smelt worse perhaps than anywhere in the world. I remember once lying off Castellamare, in the Bay of Naples, a hot evening with faint airs off the land. I thought then the odour was intolerable, but Hit was worse.

First of all there were the bitumen wells; boiling pitch bubbles to the surface, giving off sulphurated hydrogen; the odour of rotten eggs hangs heavy on the atmosphere. Then, near the town, even this is subjugated by the deadly stench of rotting carcases, drainage and refuse, littered round the walls and in the dark alleys which serve as streets. There are palm groves outside Hit, and with the quaint town standing out from among them and the broad Euphrates flowing past, the place possessed a fairy-story appearance. The retiring enemy columns were a fine quarry for airmen.

We began bombing them at dawn on the 9th, and continued till dusk; havoc was caused among troops and transport both by bombs and machine-gun fire from ground-level upwards. The deeds of the squadron could be read along the road. The enemy moved right back to Khan Baghdadi, where he took up a position on rocky heights running into the desert on the right bank of the Euphrates.

Bad weather hampered movements both on the ground and in the air. Von Drueffel, on the Persian side, received his weekly ration of bombs, and more of his native following were reported to have been killed. All this time General Cassels had been feverishly training the 11th Cavalry Brigade in the vicinity of Baghdad. The 7th Hussars and the Guides Cavalry, recently arrived from India, the 23rd Cavalry from Ahwaz, and W Battery R.H.A., with 18-pounder guns, hauled by four pairs of horses instead of the usual 13-pounder R.H.A. battery with three-pair teams.

They trained night and day as an independent brigade, and Bob Cassels, dreaming of victories to be, awaited the opportunity to lead his finely-tempered machine into action. He hoped hard 'to be sent to the Euphrates, and to get his chance before the enemy slipped away out of reach. I arrived back at Baghdad in time to play polo one afternoon, and told him the sad news of the rapid Turkish retirement to Khan Baghdadi. It looked as though for the rest of the war our energies would be confined to polo. Poor Cassels was a disappointed man.

A Baghdad "week" had been arranged: racing, polo tournament, horse show, golf tournament, football, boxing, etc. As many as could be spared came in from the desert; the G.O.C. himself captained one of the polo teams, and for four days Baghdad was a scene of sport and jollification such as it had never witnessed before. Keenness and competition were at fever heat, and concerts at night culminated the day's programme. The messes were crammed, and a special camp had been arranged for the overflow.

The final of the polo tournament was a sight that will never be forgotten. The match was watched by thousands; the 22nd Cavalry and 14th Bengal Lancers were the finalists, their teams composed of famous players. When the whistle blew at the end of the last "chukker" it was still a draw. It had been a galloping game, and the ponies were tired. Two more "chukkers" went by with widened goalposts, and still the 22nd and 14th went thundering up and down the dusty ground with the ball in the middle. The *sowars* around waved and yelled themselves hoarse with excitement. The *syces* tried to restore freshness to the soaked, bloodshot-eyed, game little ponies. Riders and ponies were almost beat, and it had been agreed that a draw should be declared if no scoring took place in the coming "chukker."

The multitude was tense with excitement when "click" went the sticks once more as the umpire threw in the ball. The air was electric; we had forgotten the war and all else for the great god Sport. With staggering ponies the 14th Lancers, a team of magnificent sportsmen of fine polo and pig-sticking fame, pressed the ball through their opponents' goalposts. The army thundered applause.

The Indian soldier is a born sportsman; *Shikar*, Love, and War, the three things that matter to all true gentlemen, are the creed of the fighting tribesman; that was the root and glorious tradition of the native army; by it the *Sowar* or *Sepoy* judged his *Sahib*, and because of this sense of fellow-feeling, of being dealt with by "men," he loved his *sahib* better than life. When this love dies it is the end of the Indian army, and modern democratic developments are hanging over it like the Sword of Damocles. Officer your wild Pathan regiments with *Babus* from the cities or second-rate Britishers, but do not expect them to follow into the Armageddon of modern warfare.

Why did Sikh, Garhwali, or Punjabi endure the exposures and tortures of the damned through all the long war? Different in race, religion, and language, they followed gladly over unheard-of seas to fight in unknown lands and foreign climates and be mowed down and maimed in thousands. Ask the *risaldar* or *sepoy* why he left all, to fight for the infidel against his brother Mahommedans: "Smith Sahib go to war, then I go to war." Our orators who preach sedition in Hyde Park would have done well to have witnessed that polo match in Baghdad.

While we exercised our muscles at Baghdad, General Brooking still followed the Turk by moving forward men and supplies on the Euphrates, for General Marshall had issued orders to drive the enemy as far as possible. Our advanced troops at Salahiyeh were already seventy miles from the railhead at Felujah. They were entirely maintained by motor-lorries, and it seemed that further forward movement would overtax the burden of the transport services.

But the new Ford convoys were proving their use, and as much motor-transport as could be spared was sent to the Euphrates. Cassels' Cavalry Brigade marched there by night, hiding during the day, and armoured cars rolled out under cover of darkness. The enemy were fourteen miles away, at Khan Baghdadi. General Brooking decided to attack the front early on 26th March, while the cavalry and armoured cars worked round the desert flank during the night, and got across the Aleppo road and his

First race meeting at Baghdad, showing cloud shadows on the desert

line of retreat. The broad principles of this operation were the same as at Ramadi; we could only pray that he would stick to his ground.

On the evening of the 24th, Hobart, brigade-major of the 8th Infantry Brigade, dined with me in Baghdad to say farewell; his division, the 3rd, were following the 7th, which had left for the Palestine front. I happened to say that I was flying out to Hit on the following morning to have a look at the enemy's position and see the squadron. I could not say more, as the impending operations were deadly secret; but it was my intention to complete the final air arrangements with the 15th Divisional Staff and the squadron on that front. To do so it seemed necessary to gain a personal knowledge of the enemy's position at Khan Baghdadi. Hobart, who had never seen the Euphrates, and who had many friends there, was keen to come out and see them before he went down-river and left the country. Accordingly, on the morning of the 28th, we set out from Baghdad in the third new D.H. 4; the fate of the other two has already been described.

The weather was cool, with the wind in the north and driving black rain clouds. The D.H. 4. forged along in the teeth of this at a comfortable 100 miles an hour. The Euphrates was eventually picked up, and then we were immersed in the fluffy fog of a rainstorm at 4,000 feet. We broke out of it with Hit astern and to our left, the country below a mass of *nullahs* and rocks. We had gone fairly low to avoid the heavy clouds; I could hear the well-known crackling of machine-guns somewhere down there on the floor, but could see no sign of life. Glancing at my instruments, the temperature of the water had suddenly gone up to boiling point; when that happens it is time to turn for home.

Then the dial went back to 0; the only possible inference from these wild fluctuations could be that there was no water left; those infernal machine-guns must have hit our radiator. Easing down the engine, I made for our lines in the hope of crashing somewhere among the rocks within reach of friends, but it was soon apparent that we were dropping too fast to clear enemy country, and the overheated engine could not be expected to revolve much longer. A thousand feet up the propeller stopped, and the sudden silence intensified the racket of machine-gun and rifle fire from below. They were hitting us now, and we could see the Turks running about on the ground.

There seemed no place where it was possible to land, but we turned up a *nullah* running down from the desert, and somehow alighted on a few yards of sand without crashing. The hills and rocks rose up all around us, and from these the fire continued, the bullets crashing through the machine and throwing up the dust. I tore at a petrol-pipe with the blackness of despair, while Hobart searched in his clothing for matches; at least we would burn the machine. Having ignited a leak we jumped clear of the machine; Turks appeared from cover and advanced cautiously, for the zone was still bullet-swept from sportsmen on the further heights. They ran in and we held up our hands.

A little officer rushed up and greeted us warmly, telling us not to be frightened, and congratulating us on being alive. But we cared neither for his remarks nor the fact that we were still alive! They led us to a shelter, which happened to be battalion H.Q., where we were politely received by a lieutenant-colonel, to whom we handed the contents of our pockets. Several other officers came in, and all chattered unceasingly while the battalion commander wrote a report, and we endeavoured to make them understand the spelling of our names and ranks. Coffee was produced, and the excited eloquence of the enemy became more voluble. They seemed pleased with their capture.

We were growing a bit bored with this, when a new officer burst in, and informed us we were to ride back with him. After much handshaking, we mounted two broken-down ponies, and, surrounded by a magnificent escort, clattered down the *wadi*. How I longed for one of my polo ponies; that ragged crew would have been left standing. *En route* we were met and ecstatically greeted by a dapper little Turkish officer, who explained that he, he alone, was responsible for our capture. He it was who commanded the machine-guns, and who had so aptly directed the barrage against us; with eighteen *mitrailleuses* on one hill, he assured us that there had been no possibility of our escape; but he expressed profound satisfaction that we were unhurt, and were we not lucky, as we would now be alive at the end of the war. So, fuming with pride and self-satisfaction, this droll specimen of the Turkish army strutted back to his *mitrailleuses*.

Rounding a corner we came upon a suspiciously British-looking bell-tent, with an unsuccessful attempt at a garden outside it. Dismounting here, we were greeted by a genial old Turk, whose benign smile disclosed two complete rows of golden teeth. This suave old gentleman did nothing but express condolence and attempt to persuade us that our lot was most fortunate.

The Germans were advancing, and Paris was being bombarded; the war would soon be over, and we should return safe to our homes in England; with this well-meant but distasteful sympathy ringing in our ears, coffee and cigarettes were handed round. He told us of his various visits to Paris, and said he intended coming to London as soon as the war was over; we must give him our addresses, and together we should have an evening's entertainment, for he had heard that the ladies were lovely in London, and the sly old *roué* winked his eye! With the utmost courtesy he bade us farewell, and we left him, his gold teeth flashing in the sunlight.

After another hour's ride the Divisional H.Q. were reached, and we were brought before Nazmi Bey, commanding the Euphrates Front. A tall, spectacled, serious-looking Turk, communication with him was impossible as he could speak no French. A smart-looking boy who talked broad Yankee arrived to interpret.

The conversation was long and flagging, for his part dwelling mostly on the German successes in France; news had reached us at Baghdad of the March offensive at Cambrai, but we were disinclined to believe that the reverse on the Western Front was as serious as they stated. Ali, the boy, seemed most friendly, and during the conversation volunteered advice regarding our answers, and kept telling us not to be frightened of the general!

Nazmi Bey was inquisitive about our aerial activity: Why did we not leave them alone for a minute? Was it fair that they should be bombed and machine-gunned night and day? What did it all mean? His questions were rather inopportune, as, knowing the plans for the morrow, it was vital to allay any suspicion that might be latent in the mind of the enemy commander.

We parried them by subtle flattery in the suggestion that, with such an opponent, the strictest vigilance was essential. The Turkish general informed us that we should probably remain in camp with him for two or three days; this suited us well, for on the morrow the British army were to move. Ali led us off to a tent; on the way we passed four German officers sitting at their mess. The Germans lived entirely by themselves; their isolation was most marked.

Later one came to interrogate us; as he approached, Ali made the astonishing announcement, "Here comes the sausage, but pay no attention to him." Our visitor proved to be the Intelligence officer; he spoke English as an Englishman, and his name was Boyes. Having been a merchant in Calcutta for fourteen years, it was curious that he should have packed up his home and belongings to return to Germany in June, 1914. As an inquisitor he was weak; he seemed kindly disposed towards us, perhaps in deference to his English forbears. The evening was cold, and our request for a little exercise being granted gave us an opportunity for a reconnaissance of our surroundings with regard to escape; but the numerous sentries, dogs, and brilliant moon extinguished any hopes.

Ali produced some soup and black bread, and informed us that he was the son of a cigarette-maker in Stamboul; he gave us his father's address, and said he would write to him to help us. He was most sympathetic and friendly; educated in an American college, his demeanour was more Occidental than Oriental. They gave us a blanket, and, settling down on the ground for the night, we had hardly got to sleep when an officer roused us at 10 p.m. and informed us that we must move.

Knowing what I did of the plans of the army, our chief aim was to keep near the front as long as possible; we argued with the Staff officer, and eventually made him wake the general to ask if we might be left till the morning, as we were very tired. The general replied that "an order was an order," and we were to move at once. So, cold, tired, and depressed, we were bundled into a wagon behind drawn curtains and, escorted by a guard of a dozen men, jolted off across the broken ground. The cold was intense, the cart had no springs, and Hobart and I were thrown up and down on the seat like peas on a drum. Although bright moonlight without, in our *palanquin* all was darkness.

A Cossack rode at each wheel, a picturesque company with their strange clothing and shaggy mounts. The nationality of our guard was surprising; we learnt that they were deserters from the Russian army. On the box sat a Turkish Jehu, whose imprecations shattered the stillness of the night as we dived almost perpendicularly into *nullahs* or pitched and tossed among the boulders. We knew not where we were going, neither did we care; the night was interminable. Dawn came at last, but in spite of brutal belabourings the mules could go no further; so, weary and numbed, we emerged and restored our circulation by marching.

High in the sky droned a British aeroplane; soon he would be back having breakfast at Hit, lucky devil! The sun rose and warmed us up, and as the blood ran more freely through the veins our spirits improved. The village of Hadithah hove in sight, and here we were taken into the *serai*, after passing through the youth of the place, who gazed open-mouthed. Our prison was the usual flat-roofed Oriental mud building, on which we were allowed to walk about.

We took careful stock of our surroundings, for we had been informed that we should spend the night here, and were determined to make a good attempt to escape. Our position was not exactly promising; outside our room a sentry was posted, there was another in the street below, and yet another on the edge of the desert who must be passed in any attempt to get away. We planned to, after dark, jump out of the window of our room on to the head of the sentry in the street, thus breaking his neck; then run for the desert.

Two Armenian doctors came to see us, and, as usual, were more friendly towards the English than towards the Turk. They promised us a meal and blankets for the night, and we obtained leave from the commandant to visit their hospital in the afternoon. This was situated in the main town of Hadithah, on an island in the Euphrates, to which we were ferried in an ancient barge. The hospital was a dismal sight: an ordinary Arab house with men lying in rows on mattresses on the floor; there was the usual complete lack of medical arrangements.

While we were there a Turk died as the result of wounds from an aeroplane bomb. The Armenians were most sympathetic, and showed us a testimonial from Haight and Hancock, expressing gratitude at their treatment a few weeks before. We induced our guard to allow us to walk round the island, thereby making further reconnaissance of the lie of the country.

So friendly were the two doctors that I decided to ask them outright what they thought of any chance of escape. To my surprise and relief they were quite open to discussion, which, however, had to be carried on in an even tone of voice so as not to attract attention.

While marching in single file through a narrow lane conversing thus disinterestedly in French, I heard Hobart, who was behind me, growl, "For God's sake, be careful," and I switched off on to another topic; when we got clear of the lane he told me that above us as we passed he had seen two German officers looking down from a veranda. The Armenians held out little hope, and we returned to our prison and former plan. Ravenous with hunger, we were looking forward to a long-promised meal, when the clatter of a horseman and a buzz of conversation below caused us to think. It was 5 p.m.; we had heard no guns, but if the betting were on Bob Cassels he should be across the enemy's line of retreat somewhere down that road; at all costs we must try to stay where we were. But, in burst the commandant, who informed us we must leave at once, and, in spite of argument and obstinacy, we were hurried downstairs and shoved into the same old cart. We started off at a gallop; in every direction were fleeing Turks; all organisation and discipline seemed to have collapsed; it was a most perfect sample of *sauve qui -pent*. With every stride our chances lessened, yet Hobart and I could but chuckle at the apparent success of our friends as demonstrated in the utter terror of the flying Orientals.

The mules that were galloping us into captivity were the same wretched animals that had dragged us through the preceding night; but now the Cossacks were flying for their lives. We wondered how far down the road were the British cavalry, and what the measure of their success. The pace gradually slackened, but it was not until midnight that we halted, and were allowed to restore our circulation by walking up and down in the moonlight. A keen wind blew across the desert, and the pangs of hunger augmented the pains of cramp.

The mules staggered on through the rest of the night, while we longed for the dawn and the warmth of the sun; eventually the cart was abandoned, and we took to our feet. By 9 a.m. we reached the outskirts of Ana; on approaching the town aeroplanes flew over and commenced bombing and machine-gunning among the houses; our escort rushed us into a narrow lane and hid us from view till we sadly watched our friends disappear towards the British lines, and then, in spite of the low ebb of our spirits, marched with a swing into the barrack-square. We realised that we were now out of reach, and prospects of escape by the desert had become remote. So we fell to planning future flight from Asia Minor; the war might go on for many years, and waste our lives in prison we would not; being a prisoner, as the Turkish general later agreed with me, is *pis que le mort*.

We were so far back at Ana, fifty miles from Khan Baghdadi, where we had been captured, that a rest at least was to be expected; we had had none for two nights and two days, and only two meagre meals. Black bread and a bowl of sour milk were brought into our room, which we devoured eagerly, and the thought of the comparison with other meals at the Ritz made us laugh. Various officials came in to look at us while this meal was in progress; they were mostly Arabs; one aroused my curiosity by the furtive way in which he several times visited us. I asked him in Arabic when he thought the war would be over, and gave him several other questions; the fellow looked as if he wanted to talk. He eventually confessed that he was sick of the war, and wished he was back at home in Baghdad; this was enlightening, and we dragged it out of him that he intended joining a caravan of blockade-runners leaving for Baghdad by the desert in a few days' time. We immediately proposed that we should accompany him; but at this he put his fingers to his lips and went out.

The thought seemed too good; hopes were at least buoyed by the fact that during the last two days we had managed twice to discuss terms of escape with the enemy. But to our dismay another officer came in and gave the order for the road once more. It seemed the climax. I shammed sick, and told them to get a doctor, explaining that I, a senior officer in his Britannic Majesty's army, was in no condition to go on, and could not possibly be treated thus. An Armenian doctor was produced, but although sympathetically inclined, our remonstrances were of no avail, and we trundled out on to the road once more.

Hobart and I each had a camel; the guard consisted of twelve Tartars on foot; a more evil-looking crowd I have never seen. A Turkish *yuzbashi* who could not speak Russian was quite useless, and entirely in the hands of the Tartars. The camels were completely out of control, as we had no head-ropes, and on the word "march" they commenced describing circles until rounded up by the Tartars, a ridiculous enough sight, though our sense of humour was near to failing. All day long we trekked across open rolling plain, a vast waste, the only relief given being some grass and wild flowers. It was difficult to remain awake in order to stay on the camel, and the hours seemed unending. The sudden mental blank after the activity of life, work, and companionship overshadowed physical discomfort, and a million devils tortured one's mind.

Our aeroplanes came over, and made good shooting; bullets flicked the grass all round, but no one was hit. On the approach of the machines the guard grew very threatening, and dragged us off our animals into *nullahs*. They kept their rifles pointed at us, and one man got so excited that I saw him pull his trigger in the small of Hobart's back; by some act of God it did not go off. One boiled with rage at being man-handled by these savages, but it was useless. An amazing thing happened after sunset; the full moon came up behind a snowy cloud and all its edges looked as if they were on fire; it was the finest moon effect I have ever seen, and made an inspiring sight; even the Tartars turned round and looked at it with awe. I told Hobart that that was our cloud with the silver lining; (by the next sunset we were back in the British lines). Long after dark a light flickered in the distance yet never seemed to get any closer; we eventually reached a mud fort, a hundred thousand miles away from anywhere on earth, without a kick left in us.

In a filthy little room we found a still filthier Armenian clerk, who went to rouse the commandant. A vision in beautiful silk pyjamas appeared, and proved to be a young Turkish officer of the German school, arrogant and annoying; but he did his best as regards the little food he had, and gave us his last thimbleful of *arak*, a native spirit. This sleek young officer seemed incongruous among his remote and filthy surroundings. He talked large of his successes in Beyrout, and was evidently a young spark of that town. The *arak* made him more arrogant and egotistical than ever; be became offensive and then boring, and eventually, at 2 a.m., when our patience was about exhausted, he lurched off to bed. They gave us a blanket, and we slept like logs on the mud floor.

The morning of the 28th found the place full of fleeing Turks and Germans from Ana, and on we went. They told us Aleppo was our destination, many more hundred miles over the limitless plain. We probably should never have got 'there, for the Tartars were getting bored; besides, the food outlook was a bit dismal. A few Germans talked to us before we left, and told us of the great battle in France, and that the British were being smashed, which we did not believe. Our aeroplanes were bombing and machine-gunning along the road, but of course could not identify us from others. As a matter of fact they had been looking for us every day, and the four we saw that morning had come out to land ahead and effect our rescue.

We were having our first wash on the banks of the Euphrates at about 11 a.m., when a Cossack galloped past shouting "*Auto!*" (automobile), but I paid no attention, as I was certain that our fellows could not come nearly as far; we did not know the extent of the defeat of the Turkish force. In fact, we had given up any idea of being rescued, under the impression that there could be nobody within fifty miles. The Tartars, however, seemed alarmed, and became threatening. We managed to cool them down, got on our camels, and went on. Suddenly there burst the regular stammer of a Maxim quite close; we looked up expecting to see another aeroplane; it was so loud and sudden that the idea flashed through our minds that an aeroplane had landed to attempt our escape, and we threw ourselves off our camels and made for the cover of the river bank.

But there, a hundred yards along the road, as large as life, was an armoured car, with others behind. I howled it to Hobart, and we went with heads down as if all the devils in hell were after us. The Tartars scattered behind the rocks under the machine-gun fire; we never looked round. The officer commanding the cars, Captain Tod, leapt out and dragged us into the turret, the men within yelling with excitement. It was beyond one's wildest dreams. We lay and panted and talked till the open plain was reached, where sniping would be impossible. There the cars halted, and we all jumped out; whiskey and bully-beef were produced—the most wonderful meal of one's life.

But for its perfect execution Tod's exploit could never have been achieved. He told us that the Cavalry Brigade were in Ana, Bob Cassels having got behind the entire Turkish force. To finish off his triumph Cassels determined to get us back, and told Tod to pursue with his armoured cars up to 100 miles; if necessary he would feed him with petrol by aeroplane. Tod came on, scattering the retreating enemy as he went; the sight of the low rakish cars terrified the Turk and Arab, who cleared off the road under cover of the rocks to let him go by. Many surrendered, and were left by the roadside without their arms; at Nahiyeh, where we had spent the night, a few bursts of machine-gun fire induced our sleek young friend to haul down the star-and-crescent and surrender the fort; the dirty Armenian informed Tod that we were only a few hours ahead, and on camels.

The utmost caution was now necessary, for the escort had only to drag us a few yards off the road and we should have been lost among the rocks, inaccessible to armoured cars; or even a surprise semi-complete would give the guards time to put a bullet through us as they made good their escape. Tod, in the leading car, a snake-like Rolls-Royce, sighted us from a hill some miles away, and crept on cannily. It must have been about this time that the Cossack had galloped past shouting *Auto!* and it was well that we had managed to quiet our guards and induced them to consider, as we honestly did ourselves, that there could not possibly be any cause for a scare. Meanwhile Tod shortened his distance; the road bending among the rocky cliffs helped him, and then he was suddenly on top of us; seated at the gun himself, cool and steady, he let fly over our heads; the rest remained with the gods, and I have told about it.

Jubilant we resumed our journey, stopping to collect various prisoners *en route*; safe in Ana, we were received ecstatically by our friends of the cavalry brigade. They had captured 5,000 prisoners, and raided the enemy's line of communication to ninety miles behind his battle-front in two days.

The battle of Khan Baghdadi had proved a second Ramadi; Subri Bey had just been superseded by Nazmi Bey for retiring from Hit; therefore, when the infantry of the 15th Division collided with Nazmi Bey on the early morning of the 26th March, he stuck to his ground instead of retiring, the front position was carried by 11 a.m., and the enemy took up a firm stand a mile north of the Khan. All this time, Cassels, with his cavalry, guns,

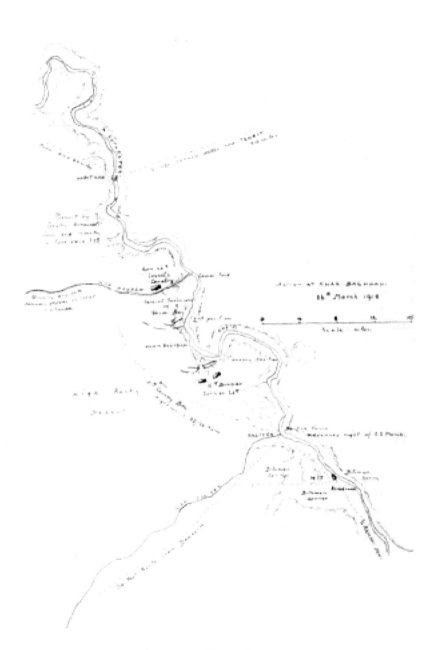

ACTION AT KHAN BAGHDADI

and armoured cars, was surmounting impossibilities in the rocky country away to the west, and working round behind the enemy. By 5 p.m. he was across the Aleppo road in rear of the Turk. (It was at 6 p.m. that the horseman had arrived at Hadithah, and we had been galloped off in the cart.) At 6 p.m. the infantry assaulted and carried the main position, taking many prisoners. Then, at 11 p.m., Nazmi made a desperate effort to break through the cavalry, but was held by Cassels' machine-guns, and lost a thousand more prisoners. At dawn the victory was complete.

A battalion standing by in Ford vans took up the pursuit with the cavalry and armoured cars, while aeroplanes mowed down the fleeing enemy further back, Hadithah was captured, and early the next morning, the 28th, the armoured cars were into Ana supported by the cavalry and motor column. The Turkish army was wiped out; of their troops on the lines of communication few got away, for the galloping pursuit did not even give them time to destroy their war stores. The road was a mass of wandering prisoners anxious to give themselves up and be delivered from the attentions of Arabs and certainty of starvation. In one cave were found a cluster of corpses murdered by the Arabs.

The pursuing column had no time to stop and collect all these prisoners, but disarmed them and passed on. A vast dump of ammunition was discovered at Ana; it took some few days to destroy; also a good store of Turkish gold. There can be no doubt that a great offensive had been planned down the Euphrates; the improved road, new bridges, arrangements for huge quantities of stores and ammunition, and irrefutable evidence in captured documents, all told the same tale, endorsed by prisoners themselves, that a Turco-German descent had once been imminent, only to be diverted by Allenby's offensive at Gaza.

General Cassels returned to report to General Brooking, and Hobart and I escorted him in an armoured car through the night, reaching Khan Baghdadi early on the morning of the 29th. It was another sleepless night, but nothing mattered now. Nazmi Bey would not believe that we had been recaptured, so we went to visit him; he was in the depth of depression and

NAZMI BEY   COLONEL TENNANT
MAJOR HOBART
COMPARING NOTES ON CAPTIVITY WITH THE TURKISH COMMANDER
ON MARCH 29TH, 1918

THE WADI WHERE WE WERE SHOT DOWN: ADVANCING BRITISH TROOPS
EXAMING THE WRECKAGE OF THE D.H.4

could say nothing; I understood how he felt. There was our old friend with the gold teeth, as cheerful and philosophic as ever; Ali, the boy, very pleased to be in British hands, and many other faces we knew; the tables were turned.

We motored on to Hit; the squadron were waiting spread out along the road, and as we arrived rushed the car and carried us off to the messes, which we had to visit each in turn. That welcome I shall never forget; the old faces that had risked their lives daily at one's order for nearly two years were there. To see their pleasure was very sweet; one has no right to say these things, but nothing can bring a man more genuine happiness than to know that his command are at his back not only from the mere force of duty; they were my best friends as well.

Then a great roar of cheering went up outside the tent, where the mechanics had collected; it was difficult to know what to say, and it was difficult to say it; but those cheers ringing in my ears were the most touching sound I had ever heard. I suppose popular heroes get used to such demonstration; when one is unused to acclamation one's vanity is perhaps keener. I learnt that Nuttall and three other pilots had gone out the day before intent on spotting us, landing on some open ground far back and holding up our escort.

They had picked two marksmen as passengers who were to shoot the nearest guards; the rest were to work the machine-guns. Frank Nuttall was certain that if he had spotted us the scheme would have been successful. It was a desperate enterprise. From Hit we flew back to Baghdad. Our mess sat up late; it was impossible to get to bed, although Hobart and I had had about five hours' sleep since the 24th; this was the 29th.

There was a Court of Enquiry as to our capture. It had been deemed undesirable that I should proceed over the enemy's lines, but the court were of the opinion that "capture was due to chances of war." So I returned to my command; Hobart caught his division at Busrah, and sailed with them to join Allenby.

During the 26th and 2 7th the squadron on the Euphrates dropped 5,550 lbs. of bombs on the enemy; these aeroplanes were continually under heavy machine-gun and rifle fire, and were often damaged, but casualties were singularly light. The moral and material effect was great. One of our machines was shot down, but Lieutenant Tanner, acting as escort, boldly followed and rescued both pilot and observer; it was a phenomenal feat for the R.E. 8 to get off the ground with four people up. No enemy aircraft were seen on this front during the fighting; they confined their attentions to the Tigris and the Diala, where they accomplished little and risked less. Owing to the wide nature of the front in Mesopotamia the chances of intercepting an odd machine were not good; they always flew at great heights, and invariably tried to avoid combat, both on our side of the lines and over their own aerodrome.

Three weeks later my orders came to leave and take up a group command at home, but by the time I reached Busrah this was changed for Headquarters in India. It was a sorry business packing up and bidding farewell to the little house in Baghdad and all the old friends in the force.

Where are you now, old companions? Scattered to the four winds, some, alas! flown to Valhalla.

ALSO FROM LEONAUR
AVAILABLE IN SOFTCOVER OR HARDCOVER WITH DUST JACKET

DOING OUR 'BIT' *by Ian Hay*—Two Classic Accounts of the Men of Kitchener's 'New Army' During the Great War including *The First 100,000* & *All In It.*

AN EYE IN THE STORM by *Arthur Ruhl*—An American War Correspondent's Experiences of the First World War from the Western Front to Gallipoli and Beyond.

STAND & FALL by *Joe Cassells*—A Soldier's Recollections of the 'Contemptible Little Army' and the Retreat from Mons to the Marne, 1914.

RIFLEMAN MACGILL'S WAR by *Patrick MacGill*—A Soldier of the London Irish During the Great War in Europe including *The Amateur Army, The Red Horizon* & *The Great Push.*

WITH THE GUNS by *C. A. Rose & Hugh Dalton*—Two First Hand Accounts of British Gunners at War in Europe During World War 1- Three Years in France with the Guns and With the British Guns in Italy.

EAGLES OVER THE TRENCHES by *James R. McConnell & William B. Perry*—Two First Hand Accounts of the American Escadrille at War in the Air During World War 1-Flying For France: With the American Escadrille at Verdun and Our Pilots in the Air.

THE BUSH WAR DOCTOR by *Robert V. Dolbey*—The Experiences of a British Army Doctor During the East African Campaign of the First World War.

THE 9TH—THE KING'S (LIVERPOOL REGIMENT) IN THE GREAT WAR 1914 - 1918 by *Enos H. G. Roberts*—Like many large cities, Liverpool raised a number of battalions in the Great War. Notable among them were the Pals, the Liverpool Irish and Scottish, but this book concerns the wartime history of the 9th Battalion – The Kings.

THE GAMBARDIER by *Mark Severn*—The experiences of a battery of Heavy artillery on the Western Front during the First World War.

FROM MESSINES TO THIRD YPRES by *Thomas Floyd*—A personal account of the First World War on the Western front by a 2/5th Lancashire Fusilier.

THE IRISH GUARDS IN THE GREAT WAR - VOLUME 1 by *Rudyard Kipling*—Edited and Compiled from Their Diaries and Papers Volume 1 The First Battalion.

THE IRISH GUARDS IN THE GREAT WAR - VOLUME 2 by *Rudyard Kipling*—Edited and Compiled from Their Diaries and Papers Volume 2 The Second Battalion.

AVAILABLE ONLINE AT **www.leonaur.com**
AND OTHER GOOD BOOK STORES

Lightning Source UK Ltd.
Milton Keynes UK
UKOW04f0058040817
306665UK00001B/57/P